The Time Value of Money

D1522187

WORKED AND SOLVED PROBLEMS

GARY E. CLAYTON, Ph.D.
Arkansas State University
State University, Arkansas

CHRISTOPHER B. SPIVEY, Ph.D.
The Citadel, Charleston, South Carolina

1978

W. B. SAUNDERS COMPANY / Philadelphia / London / Toronto

W. B. Saunders Company: West Washington Square
Philadelphia, PA 19105

1 St. Anne's Road
Eastbourne, East Sussex BN21 3UN, England

1 Goldthorne Avenue
Toronto, Ontario M8Z 5T9, Canada

Library of Congress Cataloging in Publication Data

Clayton, Gary E.
    The time value of money.

    1. Discount—Tables, etc. 2. Annuities—Tables, etc.
I. Spivey, Christopher B., joint author. II. Title.
HG1654.C64   332.8'01'51   77-11332
ISBN 0-7216-2602-5

The Time Value of Money: Worked and Solved Problems   ISBN 0-7216-2602-5

Last digit is the print number: 9 8 7 6 5 4 3 2 1

With special dedications and thanks to
Clayt, Kimberly and Brandon
and
Mary Ann, Cathy and Eric

PREFACE

This little volume, *The Time Value of Money*, represents a labor of love which has occupied the authors during the past four years. The concept of the book came out of our many discussions concerning the difficulty of devoting enough class time to this important topic—a difficulty compounded by a lack of suitable readings in the field to which we could refer our students.

Because of this, we decided that we would try to put together a reasonably comprehensive survey of the basic time value concepts—one thorough enough for a college course, yet one that would be short and concise for the interested reader to pursue on his own. In particular, we wanted a text that would minimize the mathematical approach and instead concentrate on the logic of solving the problems. The pages which follow represent our best efforts in this respect and we hope that we have made a useful addition to the literature in the field.

We owe a debt of thanks to a number of those who helped us along the way. Dr. Spivey in particular would like to express his appreciation to Dr. George Christy at North Texas State University for giving him a challenging present value problem on his comprehensive exams. If it hadn't been a challenging problem, Dr. Spivey would not have spent the next few years making up problems, many of which appear in this book.

We would also like to express our appreciation to Dr. Herbert B. Mayo at Rider College, Dr. Daniel Williams at the University of Akron, and Dr. Anthony Curley at the Wharton School, University of Pennsylvania, for their many helpful comments pertaining to the organization, content, and structure of the various chapters.

The authors acknowledge a special debt of thanks to Dr. Jonna R. Clayton for her editorial assistance throughout the numerous revisions of the manuscript. Her diligence in working and solving each of the problems has saved us much embarrassment and has greatly clarified the remaining material for the reader.

We are also indebted to two of our former graduate students, Dean Massey and David Dearman, for the many hours they spent working the problems and proofing the final manuscript. Last but not least, we would like to thank all of our former students in the College of Business at Arkansas State University who had the misfortune to take our classes when we were using early drafts of the various chapters as part of course materials.

Finally, in spite of the valuable advice and suggestions given to us during the writing of this book, we realize that some difficult passages, if not errors, may still remain. For this we apologize with the full realization that only the authors are to be blamed for any remaining oversights.

GARY E. CLAYTON

CHRISTOPHER B. SPIVEY

January, 1978

CONTENTS

CHAPTER 1

THE TIME VALUE OF MONEY

A dollar paid to you today is not worth a dollar tomorrow.

Why? Because there is an opportunity cost that is determined by the amount of interest a dollar could earn in an alternative investment. A dollar today is not worth a dollar tomorrow; it is worth more because it could be lent out or placed on deposit, and then be reclaimed with interest when tomorrow arrives.

We also know that tomorrow's dollar is not worth a dollar today. Would you pay one dollar today for a promise to receive one dollar a year from now? Probably not. After all, you could deposit $.95 in a 5¼% account and receive one dollar a year from now. Why pay a dollar today to receive a dollar one year from now when $.95 will get you the same dollar?

These two examples may seem less than profound, but they do highlight the problem at hand: *if a dollar tomorrow is not worth a dollar today, then just what is it worth?* In fact, many problems in the fields of finance, real estate, accounting, banking, insurance, and economics deal with situations in which sums of money that exist in different time periods must be compared. This is the essence of the time value problem: because the value of money changes with time, we need methods that will allow us to compare sums existing at different points in time. The comparison can be made in the distant past, the distant future, or any year in between. The point is that equivalent values of all payments must be found in a common year so that a comparison can be made.

In the case of tomorrow's dollar, which we discussed above, we know that a dollar promised next year cannot be directly compared to a dollar paid today. However, if we know that a dollar paid next year is worth $.95 today, we *can* compare today's dollar to the $.95 present value of the dollar promised next year. As long as the interest rate remains at 5¼%, today's dollar is worth a nickel more than next year's dollar.

Let's consider another example to see how the comparison could be made in the future instead of in the present. Suppose that we wanted to compare a $100 present sum to a $105 amount one year in the future. If the best alternative investment is to put the $100 in a 5¼% account that compounds the interest annually, we know that we could withdraw $105.25 at the end of one year. Now the comparison can be made: the $100 present sum is worth more than $105 one year from today—$.25 more.

Of course our conclusion might be different if some of the parameters of the problem were to change. If the interest rate were to change to 5%, the future value of the $100 deposit would be $105 and the two sums being compared in the future would be of equivalent value. The point is that we are dealing with a problem that has four variables: the value of a sum in the future, the value of a sum in the present, the interest rate, and the number of periods or years involved. As such, the problem can be reduced to a simple algebraic exercise: given values for any three of these variables, the value for the fourth can be found.

The relationship between these four variables and the four major time value concepts examined in later chapters is illustrated in Table 1-1. Note that the table has four rows and four columns, one row for each of the four variables mentioned above and one column for each of the time value concepts. As we go across the table and examine the columns, we see that in each case three of the variables are known while the fourth is not. In fact, each of the four time value concepts in the table is named after the unknown variable in the column.

TABLE 1-1. THE FOUR TIME VALUE OF MONEY CONCEPTS

Variables	Future Value	Present Value	Discounted Rate of Return	Discount Period
Value of a Sum in the Future	?	known	known	known
Value of a Sum in the Present	known	?	known	known
Interest Rate	known	known	?	known
Time (in Periods or Years)	known	known	known	?

In the following chapters, each of these time value concepts will be examined in turn. In Chapter 2, we will work with problems in which we use the value of a sum in the present, the interest rate, and the number of periods to find the value for the remaining unknown—the value of that sum in the future. This is the type of problem illustrated in the first column of Table 1-1 and is similar to the one discussed above in which we tried to find the future value of a $100 deposit in a 5% account.

In Chapter 3 we will examine the concept of present value. As we can see in the second column of Table 1-1, we will be working with problems in which we know the values for the future sum, the interest rate, and the time period, values used to find the unknown sum in the present. Present value problems involve a process called discounting—an operation similar to compounding except that we move backward in time instead of forward. For example, if we have a future sum of $105, an interest rate of 5%, and a time period of one year, we could discount the $105 future sum back to its present value, which is $100. The process of discounting can be simplified somewhat with the use of some present value tables which are developed in Chapter 4.

In Chapter 5, we examine the type of problem illustrated in the third column of Table 1-1 and work with problems in which the rate of interest, or the discount rate as it is sometimes called, is the unknown. A problem of this nature might be expressed like this: what rate of interest would be required to discount a future sum of $105 back to a present value of $100 if exactly one year separated these two values? Again our answer is 5%, but as we shall see when we get to this chapter, a number of factors can be introduced to make the solution more interesting.

Chapter 6 deals with the last time value concept in Table 1-1, that of the discount period. In this case we know everything except the amount of time that separates a present and a future sum. This time we would pose the question in this fashion: given an interest rate of 5%, how much time separates a present sum of $100 and a future sum of $105 if these sums are of equivalent value? Of course our answer in this case is one year, but the discount period would have to be longer if the interest rate were lower, or shorter if the interest rate were higher.

Finally we come to the topic of annuities, which involve a series of equal payments at regular intervals. Since many real world problems deal with multiple future payments of equal size, Chapters 7 and 8 are reserved for this topic. Like the time value concepts we have been discussing, annuities also have four variables: the interest rate, the duration or length of the annuity, the size of each annual payment, and the lump sum value of the annuity. If we are given values for any three of these factors, the fourth can be found. We will have more to say about annuities when we get to these chapters, but for now it will be sufficient to note that they involve logical extensions of the time value concepts summarized in Table 1-1. The discussion of annuities has been left to the last only because of the complexity of the problems.

In essence, the concepts involved under the general heading of "time value of money" are fairly simple and the techniques required for solution are generally straightforward. Nevertheless, without these time value techniques, it would be impossible to obtain answers to a number of everyday questions. How much, for example, should you contribute to a retirement fund if you want to receive a specific annuity when you retire? Perhaps you would like to know the rate of return on a little investment you made recently. You might even want to plan a savings program to cover some anticipated future expense and want to know how often, or how much, to deposit so that the expense will be covered when it arrives. Perhaps you are contemplating a variable mortgage for your new home and would like to know the way in which a change in the mortgage rate will affect the number, or perhaps the size, of the monthly payments. Or maybe you would like to know who got the best of the deal in 1626 when a group of Dutch settlers bought Manhattan Island from the Indians for a mere $24 worth of trinkets.

The purpose of this book is to discuss and illustrate these time value techniques with the aid of problems and graphs. The format is a simple one: we start with the common case of future value and develop each of the four time value concepts in turn. At least one chapter is devoted to each topic and within each chapter the progression of problems is from the simple to the complex. The emphasis is on understanding the nature of the solution because this is the essence of time value problems. Short cut aids, such as tables, are provided at the end of this text, but they will not be used extensively until Chapter 4. Most problems can be solved with the use of an inexpensive desk or pocket calculator and many problems are specifically designed for their use. Finally, you will find additional problems at the end of each chapter that will allow you to test your understanding of the material as you go along.

CHAPTER 2

THE FUTURE VALUE CONCEPT

The concept of future value is the first of four major time value concepts we want to examine and it is also the easiest to grasp. Essentially we are trying to find the amount to which a present sum will grow when compounded for several periods. If you deposit a dollar today, you know that at the end of one, two, three, or more years you can withdraw the deposit plus interest. The value of the deposit at any given time in the future is called its "future value," which is what this chapter is all about.

In order to examine the concept of future value, we will proceed in stages. Accordingly, our first task will be to define some terms and develop what we will call the basic time value of money equation which serves as the basis for all time value concepts listed in Table 1-1. Next we will use this time value equation to work problems in which we want to find the future value of a present sum. Finally, we will examine some additional topics, such as the use of the pocket or desk calculator and the construction and use of a future value table.

THE TIME VALUE OF MONEY EQUATION

Suppose that you deposit $100 in a bank today and you want to find the value of that deposit at the end of one year. If the deposit earns interest, its value at that time would be equal to the initial deposit *plus* the deposit *times* the interest rate. With an 8% interest rate, the value of the deposit will be $100 plus 8% of $100, or

$$\text{future value} = (\$100) + (\$100)(.08).$$

And, by factoring out the common term, we could rewrite and compute the above more simply as

$$\text{future value} = \$100\,(1 + .08) \qquad (2\text{-}1)$$

$$= \$100(1.08) = \$108.$$

Of course we could leave the deposit untouched for the second year as well. If we start the second year with $108 and it grows 8% during the year, we will end the second year with

$$\text{future value} = (\$108) + (\$108)(.08) \tag{2-2}$$

$$= \$108 (1 + .08)$$

$$= \$108(1.08) = \$116.64.$$

We could continue the procedure for any number of years and find the value of the deposit in the *nth* year, but unfortunately this would require n computations! Instead, let's go to an alternative method that gives us a general formula useful for any deposit and any number of periods. To get this formula, we start by defining the following terms:

S_0 = present value, the value of a sum of money today;

$S_1, S_2, \ldots S_n$ = the value of a sum of money at the end of periods $1, 2, \ldots n$;

r = interest or discount rate per period;

n = number of periods (usually expressed in years).

Of course, all we've done here is to shorten the notation used to identify the variables listed in Table 1-1.

If we rework the initial deposit problem above using the terms just defined, it should be evident that S_0 has a value of $100, r has a value of 8%, while n equals 1. Expression (2-1) could then be rewritten as

$$S_1 = S_0 (1 + r), \tag{2-3}$$

and, by putting the numbers back in, we get

$$S_1 = \$100 (1 + .08)$$

$$= \$100(1.08) = \$108.$$

When the deposit was left untouched the second year, we found its value, S_2, to be equal to

$$S_2 = S_1 (1 + r) \tag{2-4}$$

$$= \$108 (1 + .08)$$

$$= \$108(1.08) = \$116.64,$$

which, if still untouched at the end of year 3, would be equal to

$$S_3 = S_2 (1 + r) \qquad (2\text{-}5)$$

$$= \$116.64 (1 + .08)$$

$$= \$116.64(1.08) = \$125.97.$$

A minor problem with expression (2-5) is that we have lost sight of the initial \$100 deposit, a problem that can easily be corrected. Recall that since S_2 is equal to $S_1 (1 + r)$, we can substitute the latter term for the former in equation (2-5) to get

$$S_3 = S_1 (1 + r) (1 + r). \qquad (2\text{-}6)$$

And, since S_1 is equal to $S_0 (1 + r)$, further substitution yields

$$S_3 = S_0 (1 + r) (1 + r) (1 + r).$$

Notice that we have multiplied the expression $(1 + r)$ three times, once for each year. Instead of writing it three times (or more, in longer problems) we could use an exponent and write it only once:

$$S_3 = S_0 (1 + r)^3. \qquad (2\text{-}7)$$

Finally, since we don't want to limit ourselves to three-year problems, we can generalize to n periods instead. This gives us our basic *time value of money equation* below, where the exponent on the right stands for the number of periods separating the present and the future sums:

$$S_n = S_0 (1 + r)^n. \qquad (2\text{-}8)$$

Since the equation is arranged so that the future sum, S_n, appears on the left side of the equation, we could also call it a compound interest or, better yet, a *future value equation*. As we will see in the next section, we will be able to use the time value expression as it is written to find the future value of a present sum.

THE FUTURE VALUE OF A PRESENT SUM

In this section we are going to begin with a single sum in the present and then find its value in the future. Let's take a look at our first problem and then try to solve it using the time value equation (2-8) developed above.

Problem 2-1:

If you deposit $100 in a 9% account and leave it untouched for 10 years, what will be the future value of that account if the interest is compounded annually?

$$S_{10} = \$100 (1 + .09)^{10}$$

Solution:

The future value formula is

$$S_n = S_0 (1 + r)^n,$$

and by putting in the numbers we have

$$S_{10} = \$100 (1 + .09)^{10}$$

$$= \$100 (2.3674) = \$236.74.$$

In ten years your deposit will be worth $236.74.

That wasn't difficult, was it? Tedious, perhaps, with ten multiplications of $(1 + .09)$, but not difficult. Later in the chapter, we'll show you two ways to shorten the computation, but right now we want to concentrate on the nature of the problem and not the short cuts to the solution. Let's take a look at the figure below, which illustrates Problem 2-1 graphically.

We can see that our initial $100 deposit increased in value as we moved along the time axis. Of course, we can't always assume that the future value will be larger than the present value because it depends on the interest rate. If the interest rate is negative, the future value will be smaller than the present value. If the rate is positive, as in the case of Problem 2-1, the future value will be larger.

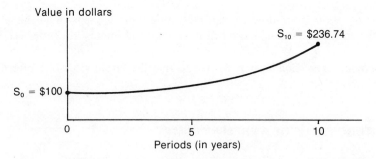

Figure 2-1. Problem 2-1: Finding the future value of a present sum.

Regardless of the sign of the interest rate or the size of the future sum, it should be evident that when solving future value problems we are simply moving *ahead* in time. In the case of Figure 2-1, S_{10} is simply later (chronologically) than S_0. Our next problem takes this observation a step further.

Problem 2-2:

In 1894 your grandfather loaned $500 to a neighbor at 12%. When the loan was paid off in 1898, how much did your grandfather collect?

$$a = 500 \left(1 + .12\right)^4$$

Solution:

First, we observe that the loan was made for a period of four years, from 1894 to 1898. Then we use our future value formula which is

$$S_n = S_0 (1 + r)^n.$$

And, by putting in the numbers we have

$$S_4 = \$500(1 + .12)^4$$

$$= \$500(1.5735) = \$786.75.$$

So your grandfather got back $786.75 after four years.

You probably noticed that in the problem above we called the $500 in 1894 the *present* value and the $786.75 in 1898 the *future* value although this all happened many years in the past. Don't let the terminology confuse you: the actual dates are unimportant, it's the four-year span that matters. By *present value* we mean the value of the loan at the beginning of the four-year term, and by *future value* we mean the value of the loan at the end of the four-year term. In solving a future value problem we move forward along the time axis from the present value to the future value—it is immaterial whether "present" means 1894, 1625, or 1984.

We want to go on to other future value problems, but before we do, let's see what would happen when interest is compounded other than on an annual basis.

Problem 2-3:

What would be the value of a $100 deposit one year from today if the 6% stated annual interest is compounded semiannually instead of annually?

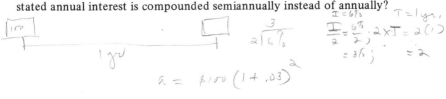

Solution:

If the interest is compounded semiannually, you will receive half of the stated annual interest, or $\frac{6\%}{2}$, in the first six months and the other half during the second six months. Since the problem involves two periods, we write

$$S_2 = \$100(1 + .03)^2$$

$$= \$100(1.0609) = \$106.09.$$

We know that if the interest were compounded annually, the value for S_n would be $106.00. Where did the extra $.09 come from? Well, if the first $3.00 interest payment was added to the account at the end of 6 months, then interest on this amount equal to $\frac{6\%}{2}$ times $3.00, or $.09, would be earned. Essentially, the $.09 is interest earned during the second period on the interest paid for the first.

This may look a bit complicated, but it's really not. Whenever the stated annual interest is compounded on any basis other than annually, simply divide the stated annual interest by the number of times the interest is compounded to find the interest per period. For the most part, as in the case of a bank or financial institution that pays interest quarterly, monthly, or daily, you will usually be told if the interest is being compounded other than annually. If you are not given this information, you can assume that the interest is compounded on an annual basis so that the length of the period, n, has a duration of one year.

In fact, whenever the stated annual interest is compounded more than once a year, the true or effective interest will always be larger than the stated annual rate. For example, suppose that the stated annual rate of 6% was compounded quarterly; then any initial deposit, S_0, would have a value of

$$S_4 = S_0(1 + \frac{6\%}{4})^4$$

$$= S_0(1.015)^4 = S_0(1.0614)$$

at the end of the year. In other words, the deposit would be 6.14% larger at the end of the year than it was at the beginning even though the stated annual interest was 6%. Likewise, any deposit left for six months in a 6% account that compounds interest monthly would have a value of

$$S_6 = S_0(1 + \frac{6\%}{12})^6$$

$$= S_0(1.005)^6 = S_0(1.0304)$$

at the end of six periods (months). In this case, the deposit would be 3.04% larger at the end of six months even though half of the stated annual interest is 3%.

By the way, future value problems needn't always be concerned with loans or sums deposited in a bank as the next problem illustrates:

Problem 2-4:

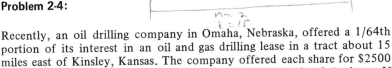

Recently, an oil drilling company in Omaha, Nebraska, offered a 1/64th portion of its interest in an oil and gas drilling lease in a tract about 15 miles east of Kinsley, Kansas. The company offered each share for $2500 and planned to drill two exploratory wells during the life of the lease. If you bought one share, how much would you have to sell your rights for two years later when the exploration lease expires in order to realize a 15% rate of return on the investment?

Solution:

Of course if the wells are dry your rights are worthless, but this is the risk that is compensated for by the unusually high 15% rate of return. To *get* this return your investment must grow just as if it were in a 15% savings account. We'll use the future value equation to find this amount in two years.

$$S_n = S_0(1+r)^n$$
$$= \$2500(1+.15)^2$$
$$= \$2500(1.3225) = \$3306.25$$

So if you sell your rights 2 years hence for less than $3306.25, you will realize less than a 15% return.

Many other future value problems, like the one below, are two-part problems and need to be separated into their component parts before they can be solved.

Problem 2-5:

You put $150 into your 5% savings account today, but you know that in 2 years you will have to withdraw $100 to buy a class ring. How much will be in your account when you graduate in 3 years?

Solution:

Since this is a two-part problem, let's do one part at a time. First of all, let's find the value of the deposit at the end of the second year before the withdrawal is made. Starting with our future value formula we get

$$S_2 = S_0(1+r)^2$$

$$= \$150(1+.05)^2$$

$$= \$150(1.1025) = \$165.38.$$

Now you withdraw the $100, leaving $65.38 to be compounded for the remaining year. (We're going to treat the second part as if it were a separate problem so we'll start over and call $65.38 the new present sum, S_0')

$$S_1' = S_0' (1+.05)$$

$$= \$65.38(1.05) = \$68.65.$$

So to work a complex problem, all we need to do is to break it down to its basic components. Many problems in this book are solved this way, so be careful.

[handwritten annotations: $n=3$ 1174.20 $n=5$ $c=.055$ $c=.075$ 1000 $S_n = 1000 (1+.055)^3 \approx 1174.20$ $S_n = \$1174.20 (1+.075)^5 \approx 1685.68$]

Problem 2-6:
Eight years ago you bought a $1000, 3-year, 5½% certificate of deposit. When it matured you bought a 5-year, 7½% certificate of deposit that matures today. If interest on the certificates were compounded annually instead of paid out, would you have enough money to buy a $2000 yacht? *[handwritten: no]*

Solution:

Obviously this is another two-part problem, the first three years and the last five years. If we start with our future value formula and solve the first part, we get

$$S_n = S_0(1+r)^n$$

$$S_3 = \$1000(1+.055)^3$$

$$= \$1000(1.1742) = \$1174.20.$$

We still have five years left, but we have a new interest rate of 7½% so we'll start over as if we had a new problem. Now our initial, or present, sum is $1174.20, which we will call S_0'. Compounding for the last five years we get:

$$S_5' = S_0' (1 + .075)^5$$

$$= \$1174.20(1.4356) = \$1685.68.$$

Simple, once you make a simple problem out of it. However, simple or not, it's not enough to buy a $2000 yacht.

Let's try another compound problem just to make sure you have mastered the method. This one is a little different because we will try to find the future value of several sums that occur in different years. $S_{n_3} = \$1000(1+.12)^3 =$

$+ S_{n_2} = \$1000 (1+.12)^2 =$

$+ S_{n_1} = \$1000 (1+.12)^1 =$

Problem 2-7: $n=3$

If you put $1000 into a 12%, 3-year finance company note today, another $1000 into a 12%, 2-year note next year, and another $1000 into a 12%, 1-year note the year after that, how much cash will you get back when these 3 notes mature in 3 years?

Solution:

Remember, break the problem down into its simple components. We have one note compounding for 3 years, one for 2 years, and one compounding for 1 year. The 3 together give us the total. If we use our future value formula,

$$S_n = S_0(1 + r)^n,$$

we can find, and then add, the values of each note at maturity:

$$\$1000(1 + .12)^3 = 1000(1.12)^3 = 1000(1.4049) = 1404.90$$

$$\$1000(1 + .12)^2 = 1000(1.12)^2 = 1000(1.2544) = 1254.40$$

$$\$1000(1 + .12)^1 = 1000(1.12)^1 = 1000(1.1200) = 1120.00$$

$$\$3779.30 = S_3.$$

When the third year arrives, your notes will mature and you will collect $3779.30. Since this amounts to a single lump sum in the third year, we can call it S_3, even though it represents the proceeds of several separate investments.

We might add that this problem is also called an annuity because it involves equal annual amounts. We will discuss annuities in more detail in Chapters 7 and 8, but you can see that the idea is really very simple.

If we wanted to draw a graph that would illustrate the solution of Problem 2-7, it would appear as in Figure 2-2. Note that the first sum was compounded for three years, the second for two, and the third was compounded for one. Then the three sums were added together to find the total value of $3779.30. In fact, Figure 2-2 is really only a minor variant of Figure 2-1 earlier in the chapter. We are still moving *forward* along the time axis; the only difference is that we have added sums in years one and two to the one in year zero.

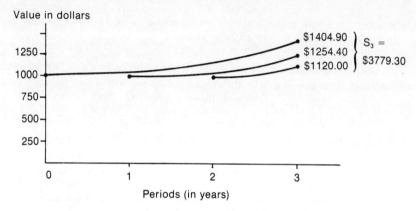

Figure 2-2. Problem 2-7: Finding the future value of multiple sums.

Now that we've had a little practice with future value problems, it's time to move on to some additional topics in this chapter. First, however, we want to tell you one of our favorite tales. Since it concerns future value, we'll put it in the form of a problem.

Problem 2-8:

During the late 1950s, there was a science fiction story about a man who was building a time machine and needed $50,000 to complete it. Every cent he could scrape together totaled $4750. His partially finished machine would travel only ten years into the past and back, and he wanted to finish it to allow travel any distance into the past or future. The time was 1958, and savings accounts between 1948 and 1958 paid 4%. How did he manage to pay for his project?

Solution:

Of course! Using his partially constructed machine, he took his $4750 back to 1948, opened a 4% savings account and returned to 1958 to collect it. But, he didn't collect $50,000, only $7030.95, since

$$S_n = S_0(1 + r)^n$$

$$= \$4750(1.04)^{10}$$

$$= \$4750(1.4802) \quad = \$7030.95.$$

Too bad! The world could sure use another time machine, but he couldn't get the capital together, right?

Wrong, that's all he collected on his *first* trip. On his *second* trip. . . .

Actually, our hero never did complete the task because on his second trip he was arrested as a rather incompetent counterfeiter trying to pass 1953 series bills in 1948. The authorities were, however, impressed with the quality of his engraving work.

ADDITIONAL TOPICS

As we have just seen, the concept of future value is relatively simple. We have to be careful whenever the interest is compounded on any basis other than annual, and sometimes the problem must be broken down into its component parts before it can be solved. If anything makes the topic a little difficult, it is that the solution can become tedious whenever more than one year is involved. Fortunately, however, there are ways to overcome this obstacle and we'll take a look at two of them here.

The first way to simplify some of the computation is with the use of an inexpensive desk or pocket calculator.* In fact, the problem becomes relatively simple if your calculator has a constant feature† or an exponential power key as illustrated by the following problem:

Problem 2-9:

When we worked the first problem in this chapter, we had to compute the value for the term $(1 + .09)^{10}$ before it could be multiplied by the $100 present sum. How would you solve this with your calculator?

Solution:

The first step is to convert $(1 + .09)^{10}$ to $(1.09)^{10}$ and then execute the following steps:

---

*Most inexpensive calculators will use either arithmetic (business) or algebraic logic. Calculators with arithmetic logic will have ⊞ and ⊟ keys while those with algebraic logic will have separate ⊞, ⊟, and ⊟ keys. As for the placement of the decimal, many business or arithmetic calculators will allow you to predetermine the number of decimal places while algebraic calculators tend to favor a floating decimal. Regardless of the type of calculator you may have, take the time to become familiar with it and be sure you know how to use its features. The steps outlined above and in subsequent problems will work for most calculators on the market today.

†Some of the algebraic calculators have a built-in constant feature which is used simply by depressing the ⊟ key. Others have a key labeled $\boxed{k}$ and still others have a separate $\boxed{k}$ key. For the remainder of the text, we will assume that our algebraic calculator has a built-in, or omnipresent, constant feature.

Arithmetic

1. set for floating decimal
2. constant key on
3. enter 1.09 (for 1 + 9%) in the keyboard
4. press the ☒ key
5. press the ⊞ key *nine* times
6. 2.3674 (rounded off) appears in the display

Algebraic

1. enter 1.09 (for 1 + 9%) in the keyboard
2. press the ☒ key
3. press the ☐ key *nine* times
4. 2.3674 (rounded off) appears in the display

or:

1. enter 1.09 in the keyboard
2. press the y^x exponential key
3. enter 10 in the keyboard
4. press the ☐ key
5. 2.3674 (rounded off) appears in the display

Now that you have the value for $(1 + .09)^{10}$, simply multiply this by the $100 present sum and you will have the future value of $100, which is $236.74.

As you can see, the calculator can be used to simplify some of the computations. You might even want to use your calculator to solve problems as we go along, but you should expect an occasional variation in your answer since we have rounded our values to four decimal places. For example, in the case of Problem 2-9, which we just worked out, the fact that the number in the display was not rounded off to four decimal places did not affect our answer. One hundred dollars times 2.3674 (Problem 2-1) is $236.74, just as is $100 times 2.3673637 (the number that appears in the display in Problem 2-9). This is not the case when the present sum is larger, say $1,000,000. If we reworked both problems using this larger present sum, we would find future values of $2,367,400.00 and $2,367,363.70, respectively. The difference is not significant, but it is there and might tend to confuse matters unless you are alerted to this problem ahead of time.

The calculator is one tool that can be used to shorten some of the computation, and the use of a future value table is another. We're going to construct such a table, but first we need to define a new term. We're going to call the $(1 + r)^n$ portion of the time value equation a *future value factor* or *fvf* for short:

$$fvf = (1 + r)^n. \tag{2-9}$$

If we rewrite the time value equation using this definition, it should be evident that the product of the factor and the present sum will yield the future sum:

$$S_n = S_0 (1 + r)^n$$

$$= S_0 \text{ (fvf)}. \tag{2-10}$$

Now we can go ahead with the construction of a future value table. All we need to do is compute the value for the term $(1 + r)^n$ for the more commonly used interest rates and time periods and arrange these values in a convenient table.

For example, suppose that we are working with a 9% interest rate. Regardless of the problem, we can see that any sum deposited for one period would have to be multiplied by $(1 + .09)^1$ or by $(1 + .09)^2$ if left for two periods. If the interest rate were 10%, the deposit would be multiplied by $(1 + .10)^1$ if left for one period, $(1 + .10)^2$ if left for two periods, or $(1 + .10)^3$ if left for three. Since the progression is the same for any rate of interest and for any number of periods, we could construct a table of future value factors as in Table 2-1.

TABLE 2-1. CONSTRUCTION OF A FUTURE VALUE TABLE

Periods	9%	10%	11%	12%
1	$(1 + .09)^1 =$ 1.0900	$(1 + .10)^1 =$ 1.1000	$(1 + .11)^1 =$ 1.1100	$(1 + .12)^1 =$ 1.1200
2	$(1 + .09)^2 =$ 1.1881	$(1 + .10)^2 =$ 1.2100	$(1 + .11)^2 =$ 1.2321	$(1 + .12)^2 =$ 1.2544
3	$(1 + .09)^3 =$ 1.2950	$(1 + .10)^3 =$ 1.3310	$(1 + .11)^3 =$ 1.3676	$(1 + .12)^3 =$ 1.4049
4	$(1 + .09)^4 =$ 1.4116	$(1 + .10)^4 =$ 1.4641	$(1 + .11)^4 =$ 1.5181	$(1 + .12)^4 =$ 1.5735
5	$(1 + .09)^5 =$ 1.5386	$(1 + .10)^5 =$ 1.6105	$(1 + .11)^5 =$ 1.6851	$(1 + .12)^5 =$ 1.7623

The advantage of the future value table is simply that some of the computation is done for you. For example, when we were trying to figure how much your grandfather would get back on his loan when it was repaid in 1898 (Problem 2-2), we could have looked in the table under the 12% column on the 4-period row and found 1.5735. We could have then multiplied $500 by this factor instead of by $(1 + .12)^4$ and saved some computation, since 1.5735 *is* $(1 + .12)^4$ already computed. The table would have helped in the same way when we were figuring out our finance company note problem (Problem 2-7) earlier.

By the way, the construction of a future value table can be easily done with your desk or pocket calculator, especially if it has a constant key:

Problem 2-10:

Using your electronic calculator, construct a partial future value table for periods 1 through 6, using 12% as your interest rate.

Solution:

In order to compute the future value factors for periods 1 through 6 at 12%, you will have to execute the following steps:

Arithmetic	Algebraic
1. set for floating decimal	1. enter 1.12 (for 1 + 12%)
2. constant key on	2. press $\boxed{x}$ key
3. enter 1.12 (for 1 + 12%)	3. press the $\boxed{=}$ key *five* times
4. press the $\boxed{x}$ key	
5. press the $\boxed{\pm}$ key *five* times	

Every time you press the equals key the future value factor will appear in the display. All you have to do is mentally round off each answer to four decimal places and write it down. (Note that we did not try to use the exponential key on the algebraic calculator in this exercise. We could use the key to find any single factor, but unless the calculator also has a constant feature, and many do not, the intervening factors would not be displayed and could not be recorded.)

   If you are working with a negative, instead of a positive, interest rate, just use a negative value for r in the future value equation. For example, a rate of −12% would mean a value of .88 in place of 1.12 in the problem above. However, when you use your calculator to construct a table such as this, always round off each answer as you write it down. If you try to round off each answer as it appears in the display by restricting the decimal to four places, a small rounding error may enter the problem and distort the figures in later time periods.

   Now that we know how to use the calculator to construct a future value table, let's return to Table 2-1 and use it to solve a problem.

Problem 2-11:

You are trying to sell your heirloom pocket watch handed down from your great-great-grandfather. A jeweler has appraised the watch at $7 and has offered to buy it for that. Your brother back home in Reykjavik has a standing offer of $10 for the watch, but you will not return home for another 4 years. You rather desperately need $7 now, but you could borrow it at 10%. What do you do: sell now or borrow the money and sell later to repay the loan?

Solution:

First of all, we turn to the table and find the future value factor for 4 periods at 10%. Having found this value of 1.4641, we use expression (2-10) to find the cost of the $7 loan in 4 years:

$$S_n = S_0 \, (fvf)$$

$$= \$7(1.4641) = \$10.25.$$

If you borrow $7 today, you will have to repay $10.25 at the end of 4 years. The $10 your brother would pay in 4 years would not be enough to cover your loan, so sell now for $7.

A future value table is a handy thing to have, isn't it? Obviously, any table with enough periods and interest rates would be of considerable usefulness when solving future value problems. Nevertheless, for reasons that will become clear later, we have decided that this book does not need a future value table. Instead, we included another table that will work just as well—the *present* value table—but we'll have to wait until Chapter 4 to find out how to use a present value table to solve a future value problem.

SUMMARY

This concludes the chapter on future value, a chapter concerned with finding the amount to which an initial dollar sum would grow as it is compounded forward through time. The technique is straightforward and is based on the simple time value of money equation below:

$$S_n = S_0(1 + r)^n.$$

We also defined the $(1 + r)^n$ term in the time value equation as the future value factor, or fvf, which allows us to write the future value equation as:

$$S_n = S_0 \, (fvf).$$

As long as you remember that we are talking about interest rates and time in terms of periods, rather than years, you should have no trouble. For example, if the interest is compounded on any basis other than annual, simply divide the stated annual interest rate by the number of times it is compounded and you will have the interest for that period.

In fact, there really aren't any secrets when it comes to computing the future value of a given sum. Keep in mind that the actual beginning and ending dates, as in the grandfather problem, are of no consequence as long as you are moving *ahead* in time. Other problems, such as the one involving the class ring, need to be broken down into component parts before they can be solved.

When it comes to simplifying some of the computation, the inexpensive pocket calculator can be extremely useful if it has a constant key or an exponential power key. Many of the problems in later chapters will be solved with the use of such a calculator, so take the time to become familiar with yours if you have one. Another device that can be used to simplify the computation is a table that we developed in the previous section. As mentioned earlier, this book does not have a future value table because we will develop a present value table later in Chapter 4 that can be used to solve the same type of problem. Since we won't return to future value problems for a few chapters, we can wait until Chapter 4 to find out how to use it.

Finally, you will find it worthwhile to try to solve the additional problems that can be found at the end of each chapter. These problems are modeled after the worked and solved problems found in the text and will give you an opportunity to test your understanding of the concepts developed in the chapter.

ADDITIONAL PROBLEMS

1. Problem 2-3 dealt with a $100 deposit in a 6% account; how much would you have at the end of 1 year if the interest were compounded quarterly instead of semiannually?

    Answer: $106.14

2. In Problem 2-5, how much would you have at graduation if you had a 6% account instead of a 5% account?

    Answer: $72.65

3. Using your pocket calculator, find the future value factor for 6.75% in the ninth period.

    Answer: 1.8002

4. If you buy a piece of land now for $250,000, what would you have to sell it for in 3 years to earn an 11% return on your investment? (Hint: use Table 2-1.)

    Answer: $341,900

5. *Bacillus megaterium* colonies will grow about 2% per minute at 34°C when proper nutrients are present and other biological conditions are right. If a colony with a population of 10,000 cells is incubated for 30 minutes, how many cells would you expect to find? (Hint: one period = one minute.)

    Answer: 18,114

6. On a visit to the Near East, you are approached in the streets by an itinerant merchant offering to sell you a chip of Tutankhamun's wooden salad bowl for 20 shekels. If the king was entombed with his treasures (including his salad bowl) about 3000 years ago, and if the radioactive isotope carbon-14 found in organic material has a naturally occurring radiation level of 2000 millicuries per gram that *decreases* roughly 12% each millennium after death, what level of radiation would you expect to find in the wooden salad bowl fragment? (Hint: the periods used are millennia, not years.)

   Answer: 1363 millicuries per gram

7. A leading newspaper *incorrectly* reported a 12% annual rate of inflation based on a recent 1% monthly increase in the consumer price index. What is the correct annual rate of increase? (Hint: there are 12 periods in this problem.)

   Answer: 12.68%

CHAPTER 3

THE PRESENT VALUE CONCEPT

In the previous chapter we found the future value of a sum of money deposited or loaned out for a specified period of time. In this chapter we pose a similar question, but work it "backward," so to speak. Instead of starting with a present sum to find its value in the future, we will start with a sum in the future and try to find its value in the present. This type of problem is illustrated in the second column of Table 1-1 developed earlier; the known variables are now the future sum, the interest rate, and the amount of time involved. The unknown variable we seek is today's value of that future sum.

This is another way of dealing with the problem of comparing sums at different points in time discussed earlier in Chapter 1. Which is worth more, a given sum today or a different sum twelve months from now? Of course we can't compare two sums unless the comparison is made in the same year. We know that the first could be compounded ahead for one year so that the comparison can be made at that time, but why can't we "*discount*" the second sum back to today so that the comparison can be made in the present? The comparison can be made in either year, but we live in the present and that's why present value is commonly used.

The remainder of this chapter deals with the present value concept which, as we shall see, is relatively uncomplicated, with the possible exception of problems that have more than one future sum.

THE PRESENT VALUE OF A FUTURE SUM

To illustrate, suppose that your rich uncle's will leaves you exactly $236.74 to be paid ten years from today. What then is the value today of that future sum, i.e., the present value of $236.74? Fortunately, the answer to the question is not too difficult because of the work we did in the previous chapter. In fact, it turns out that the time value equation (2-8) can be of some assistance.

To understand how, we only need to realize that equation (2-8) is nothing more than a simple algebraic expression with four variables: S_0, S_n, r, and n. If we have values for any three variables, the value for the fourth can be determined. This is what we did in the last chapter; we knew the values for all the terms except S_n, which we then proceeded to find. In this chapter we'll do the same thing except that we'll be looking for the value of S_0.

If we attempt to use the time value equation (2-8) developed in the last chapter,

$$S_n = S_0 (1 + r)^n,$$

we immediately notice a problem. If we are trying to find the value of S_0, we should rearrange the equation so that the unknown variable appears by itself and all the known terms appear on the other side. Naturally, all we need to do is divide both sides by $(1 + r)^n$ to get

$$S_0 = \frac{S_n}{(1 + r)^n}. \qquad (3\text{-}1)$$

This is what we will call our *present value* equation.

Now we can go ahead with the problem. We know the time period is 10 years and the value at the end of that period is $236.74. If we assume an interest, or discount, rate of 9%, we can use the three known values to find the fourth:

$$S_0 = \frac{S_n}{(1 + r)^n}$$

$$= \frac{\$236.74}{(1 + .09)^{10}}$$

$$= \frac{\$236.74}{(2.3674)} = \$100.$$

This looks suspiciously like Problem 2-1, doesn't it? Actually, it is Problem 2-1; all we have done here is to work it "backward." That is, we have moved backward along the time axis, a technique generally known as *discounting*. Perhaps the best way to contrast present value with future value is to first study and then compare Figure 3-1 with Figure 2-1 in the previous chapter.

Instead of leaving $100 in the bank for 10 years and letting it grow to $236.74 as we did in Problem 2-1, this time we have $236.74 ten years in the future and discount it back to the present. Again, the only difference between the two problems is the direction of movement along the time axis:

When we are computing *future value*, we are moving ahead in time; when we are computing *present value*, we are moving backward in time.

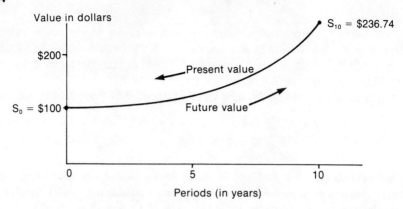

Figure 3-1.   A comparison of present and future values.

The magnitude of the present value is also dependent on the size of the discount rate. The present value of a future sum will decrease if the discount rate rises and increase if the discount rate falls. The reasons for this are not hard to understand, but the explanation will be a little clearer if we work another problem first.

Problem 3-1:

What is the present value of your $236.74 inheritance if the discount rate falls to 7%?

Solution:

The present value formula is

$$S_0 = \frac{S_n}{(1+r)^n},$$

and, by putting in the numbers, we get

$$S_0 = \frac{\$236.74}{(1+.07)^{10}}$$

$$= \frac{\$236.74}{1.9672} = \$120.34.$$

The present value of the inheritance *increases* to $120.34 from the $100 amount computed earlier when the discount rate goes *down* to 7% from 9%.

This makes sense, doesn't it? If it doesn't, think of it this way: if we had a present sum and were letting it grow to some future value, a lower rate of interest would mean that the sum would grow at a *slower* rate. Or, at 7%, we have to start with *more* than we would at 9% if we want to end up with $236.74 in 10 years. At 7%, we have to start with $120.34. A future sum being discounted back to the present, in this case at a lower rate of discount, means that the value of the sum will shrink at a *slower* rate as we move closer to the present. Figure 3-2 below illustrates both of these changes:

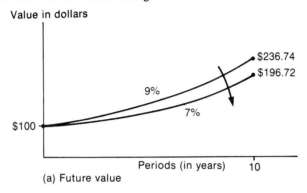

(a) Future value

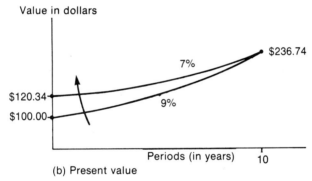

(b) Present value

Figure 3-2.   Impact of a decrease in the interest rate from 9% to 7% on future and present values.

In each case, the effect of a lower rate of interest (or discount) was to cause the time-path between the initial and the terminal values to become *flatter*. If the interest rate went up the curve would become *steeper*.

Since we'll be doing a number of problems in this chapter, let's try one problem with your calculator:

Problem 3-2:

In the solution to the last problem, we had to simplify the following expression:

$$S_0 = \frac{\$236.74}{(1 + .07)^{10}}.$$

How would you go about solving this with your calculator?

Solution:

If your calculator divides by a constant there is no problem, simply execute the following steps:

Arithmetic	Algebraic
1. set for floating decimal	1. enter $236.74
2. constant key on	2. press ÷ key
3. enter $236.74	3. enter 1.07 (for 1 + 7%)
4. press the ÷ key	4. press = key *ten* times
5. enter 1.07 (for 1 + 7%)	or:
6. press the ⊞ *ten* times.	1. enter 1
	2. press ÷ key
	3. enter 1.07 (for 1 + 7%)
	4. press y^x key
	5. enter 10
	6. press x key
	7. enter $236.74
	8. press the = key.

The answer should be $120.35. (The $.01 difference between this solution and the one in Problem 3-1 is due to rounding.)

Now you're ready to try a few more problems, but this time we'll use the present value equation (3-1) to find our answer.

Problem 3-3:

You are a minister of exports for the Republic of Maduras, but you would like to be President (or rich, as a consolation prize). You plan to finance a coup three years from today that will cost five million dollars. In exchange for a permit to export bananas without paying an export tax, how large a consulting fee must you receive today from Consolidated Fruit Company in the form of a deposit in your numbered Swiss bank account that pays 4% annual interest?

Solution:

In other words, if you want $5,000,000 in 3 years, you have to start now with what? Let's start off with our present value equation:

$$S_0 = \frac{S_n}{(1+r)^n} \ ,$$

and fill in the values to get

$$S_0 = \frac{\$5,000,000}{(1+.04)^3}$$

$$= \frac{\$5,000,000}{1.1249} = \$4,444,839.54.$$

Of course, if you could find a bank account with a higher yield, you could lower your consulting fee.

You might try this problem again using your calculator as we did in Problem 3-2, but if you do you'll arrive at an answer of $4,444,981.79 instead of the one we just found. Your new answer will be different because your calculator was set for a floating decimal, whereas in Problem 3-3 we rounded the denominator (1.1249) to four decimal places.

Here's a little problem that just might happen to anybody, even you:

Problem 3-4:

You own a five-gallon gas can that happens to be full of gas. Two motorists run out of gas in front of your home; the first offers to pay you $25 now in exchange for the gas, and the second bids $35 paid 5 years from now with his mint-condition spare tire held as security. If the money would be kept in your 5% savings account, which offer would you accept?

Solution:

We know that $35 in 5 years is not worth $35 today, but what *is* it worth? Since present value is only compound interest looked at backwards, another way of stating the question would be: "What amount invested today would grow to $35 in 5 years?" The discount rate, of course, is the 5% that our savings account pays. Using the present value equation, we write

$$S_0 = \frac{S_n}{(1+r)^n}$$

$$= \frac{\$35}{(1+.05)^5}$$

$$= \frac{\$35}{1.2763} = \$27.42.$$

Obviously, the second motorist made the better offer. If the money is worth 5% to us, the well-secured promise of $35 five years hence has a present value of $27.42, which is greater than the $25 alternative.

By the way, there was another way to answer the problem. We could have compounded $25 for 5 years at 5% and then made the comparison in the fifth year. $25 in 5 years would amount to $31.91, which is still less than the $35 the second motorist would have paid. Let's try another one:

Problem 3-5:

If your rich uncle holds your IOU for $5000 due in 3 years, what would you be willing to offer him now if you wanted to redeem it? If you do not redeem it, you plan to purchase a 3-year certificate of deposit yielding 7¾%.

Solution:

You know you will have to shell out $5000 in 3 years and you know you can invest your money now at 7¾%, so it's a matter of determining how much money *now* will become $5000 in 3 years. Again, the formula is

$$S_0 = \frac{S_n}{(1+r)^n}$$

$$= \frac{\$5000}{(1+.0775)^3}$$

$$= \frac{\$5000}{1.2510} = \$3996.80.$$

You would be willing to offer your uncle up to $3996.80 to redeem your IOU.

But wait, we're not finished with the rich uncle problem! We forgot that banks don't usually issue certificates of deposit in $3996.80 amounts.

Problem 3-6:

Would you be better off redeeming the IOU for $3996.80 or buying the 7¾% CD now and paying off the IOU when it becomes due? Bear in mind that banks like to sell CDs in round amounts and a $4000 CD is as close as you can get to $3996.80.

Solution:

If you took the $4000 and bought the CD, in three years (remember, this is now a *future value* problem) you would have

$$S_n = S_0(1 + r)^n$$

$$= \$4000(1.0775)^3$$

$$= \$4000(1.2510) \quad = \$5004.00.$$

After you paid off your uncle, you would have $4.00 in change left over.

Your alternate course of action would be to pay your uncle the $3996.80 and keep $3.20 in change. Which is worth more, the $4.00 in change three years from today or the $3.20 in change today? Let's discount $4.00 at 7¾% and see what happens.

$$S_0 = \frac{\$4.00}{(1.0775)^3}$$

$$= \frac{\$4.00}{1.2510} = \$3.20$$

How about that! It really doesn't make any difference—the present value of $4.00 discounted at 7¾% *is* $3.20.

Every now and then we all get the urge to speculate in real estate. Now it's your turn:

Problem 3-7:

You are considering the purchase of a 2½ acre lot near Interstate 35-E just north of Dallas, Texas. The lot is located next to a small manufacturing firm whose financial vice president, a friend of yours, has told you of the company's planned plant expansion three years from now. Further analysis of local industry and real estate prices leads you to believe that you could sell the property for $10,000 in three years. If the lot is listed for $7000, and if you have several 3-year treasury notes yielding 8%, should you liquidate enough notes to buy it?

Solution:

Since your capital is presently yielding 8%, you want to know if your real estate venture can be expected to do as well or better. Simply discount the $10,000 at 8% for 3 years and find out.

$$S_0 = \frac{S_n}{(1 + r)^n}$$

$$= \frac{\$10,000}{(1 + .08)^3}$$

$$= \frac{\$10,000}{1.2597} = \$7938.40$$

Yes, buy! You could pay as much as $7938.40 for the lot and still get an 8% return on your investment if — *if* you can sell the lot for $10,000. There is a very real risk that you won't. This real estate venture is a speculation, whereas your treasury note is the lowest risk investment available; the *standard* of safety. If, on the other hand, you demanded a 5% *risk premium* (a return 5% greater than a "risk-free" investment) to compensate you for the additional risk of the real estate speculation, how would your decision be affected? To find out, just tack your 5% risk premium onto your 8% risk-free rate to get a 13% expected yield. If you can't get the 13% yield, you are not interested. So, by discounting the $10,000 at 13% for 3 years you find

$$S_0 = \frac{S_n}{(1 + .13)^3}$$

$$= \frac{\$10,000}{1.4429} = \$6930.49.$$

No, don't buy! You would not pay more than $6930.49 for the property. The higher purchase price would give a yield lower than 13%, *even if* you sell for the expected $10,000.

Did you notice the inverse relationship between the change in the discount rate and the change in the present value in the above problem? This is exactly the same kind of change we diagrammed in Figure 3-2b earlier in the chapter. Well, so much for your plunge into real estate; here's one involving a future sum that must be discounted on a monthly basis:

Problem 3-8:

Your fraternity brother, mentor, and big man on campus just paid back a loan he obtained from you seven months ago. Because of his credit standing at the time the loan was made, you were able to make him an offer he couldn't refuse: 15% annual interest compounded monthly! If he paid you $92.72, how much did he originally borrow?

Solution:

The solution to this problem is similar to the one in Problem 2-3. Since there are 12 monthly periods in a year, the interest is $\frac{15\%}{12}$ or 1.25% for each of the 7 periods.

$$S_0 = \frac{S_n}{(1+r)^n}$$

$$= \frac{\$92.72}{(1+.0125)^7}$$

$$= \frac{\$92.72}{1.0909} = \$84.99$$

Actually, the loan was for $85 but we lost a penny when we rounded off.

As you can see, there's really no problem in discounting a future sum even if the stated annual interest is compounded other than annually. We simply divide the stated annual interest by the number of times per year the interest is compounded, and then solve the problem.

One final topic we should look at before we leave this section is the case in which the discount rate is negative, as in the problem below.

Problem 3-9:

It so happens that you are anxiously awaiting the design, manufacture, and marketing of a fuel-less, wind-powered automobile that is expected to be completed in four years. It has a set delivery price of $10,000, but in order to assure delivery money must be deposited today in a non-interest-paying escrow account that charges a 4% annual service fee. Since the escrow account must have $10,000 in four years, how much must you put into the account today?

Solution:

No interest this time; instead we have a fee. Your money is shrinking at the rate of 4% a year, as if we had a negative interest rate. Well, if the money is shrinking at 4%, we can use our present value equation to find the size of today's deposit:

$$S_0 = \frac{S_n}{(1+r)^n}$$

$$= \frac{\$10,000}{(1 - .04)^4}$$

$$= \frac{\$10,000}{.8493} = \$11,774.40.$$

If r is equal to a −4%, you must deposit $11,774.40 in the escrow account today in order to have $10,000 in 4 years.

Essentially, negative discount rates are easily handled; we simply use the present value equation with a negative value for r instead of a positive one. However, you should realize that we could not solve the problem by compounding the $10,000 ahead for four years at 4% in order to find the amount of the deposit. If we had tried to work it this way, we would have found an answer of $11,698.59, which is not the answer we found above.

At first this may seem confusing, but it turns out that shrinking and growing at 4% is not the same thing. When something grows at 4%, it grows at an increasing rate; when something shrinks at 4%, it shrinks at a decreasing rate. As long as one is not the mirror image of the other, we must treat negative rates of growth by using a negative value for r in the time value equation. Now for a new topic.

THE PRESENT VALUE OF MULTIPLE FUTURE SUMS

Each of the above problems involved a single sum, S_n, in the future. Now we want to try some different problems, involving several future sums. As we shall see, the problems have more parts, but they really aren't any more complicated.

Problem 3-10:

You are attending a state university, and in a recent interview the registrar advised you that your status as an in-state resident was disallowed. Because of this, your tuition costs will be $1100 higher each year starting next year, the beginning of your sophomore year. If your four-year education has been fully funded by your family in a 6% savings account, how much should you add to the account today to assure that your education will continue fully funded for its last three years?

Solution:

You have three years left to fund so the question is this: how much more money do you need to deposit now in your 6% savings account to fund the additional $1100 payment in one year for your sophomore year, in two years for your junior year, and in three years for your senior year? You *cannot* simply add the three $1100 payments together because they occur in different years. Instead, each must be discounted to the present and *then* added if you are to find the size of today's deposit that will fully fund this increase in tuition costs.

We have three future sums to be discounted, and since we need to use the present value equation (3-1) three times, let's save a little space and set the problem up this way:

$$S_0 = \frac{S_1}{(1+r)^1} \quad + \quad \frac{S_2}{(1+r)^2} \quad + \quad \frac{S_3}{(1+r)^3} \qquad (3\text{-}2)$$

$$= \frac{\$1100}{(1+.06)^1} \quad + \quad \frac{\$1100}{(1+.06)^2} \quad + \quad \frac{\$1100}{(1+.06)^3}$$

$$= \frac{\$1100}{1.06} \quad + \quad \frac{\$1100}{1.1236} \quad + \quad \frac{\$1100}{1.1910}$$

$$= \$1037.74 \quad + \quad \$979.00 \quad + \quad \$923.59 \quad = \$2940.33.$$

A deposit today of $2940.33 in a 6% savings account will allow a withdrawal of $1100 at the end of each of the next three years and leave nothing after the third withdrawal.

For the first time in this chapter we've encountered a situation in which we had to deal with several future values at the same time, a common occurrence in the real world. This didn't really pose a problem since all we had to do was compute the present value of each future payment and add them together, an operation we summarized in expression (3-2) above. Since we'll be faced with similar problems later on, it will help if we generalize expression (3-2) so that it appears as follows:

$$S_0 = \frac{S_1}{(1+r)^1} \quad + \quad \frac{S_2}{(1+r)^2} \quad + \ldots + \quad \frac{S_n}{(1+r)^n} . \qquad (3\text{-}3)$$

This is the most popular way to express the present value equation since it can deal with more than one future sum. This formula tells us that any number of future sums can be discounted back to the present, where they can be added to obtain S_0, our total present value.

Another way we can use the generalized present value equation (3-3) is to compute the market price of a bond.

Problem 3-11:

What is the market price of a $1000, 4-year, 6% bond when the yield to maturity (discount rate) is 8%?

Solution:

Since the market price of a bond is equal to the present value of the future income stream generated by the bond, we must first establish the income stream and then find its present value.

Our bond is paying 6%, so we can assume that the holder of the bond will receive an annual interest payment of $60. (Normally interest payments on bonds are made semiannually, but for simplicity we will assume that the payment is made at the end of each year.) In addition to the four annual payments of $60, the principal will be paid back in the last year. This gives us a future income stream that looks like this:

Years	Future Income	
1	$60	$(= S_1)$
2	60	$(= S_2)$
3	60	$(= S_3)$
4	60 + 1000	$(= S_4)$

We'll start with the present value equation (3-3) and discount the future income stream at 8% which is the yield to maturity.

$$S_0 = \frac{S_1}{(1+r)^1} + \frac{S_2}{(1+r)^2} + \cdots + \frac{S_n}{(1+r)^n}$$

$$= \frac{\$60}{(1+.08)^1} + \frac{\$60}{(1+.08)^2} + \frac{\$60}{(1+.08)^3} + \frac{\$1060}{(1+.08)^4}$$

$$= \frac{\$60}{1.08} + \frac{\$60}{1.1664} + \frac{\$60}{1.2597} + \frac{\$1060}{1.3605}$$

$$= \$55.56 + \$51.44 + \$47.63 + \$779.13 = \$933.76$$

The market price of the bond is $933.76. Of course, bond prices aren't quoted this way in the real world; the quote would be 93 3/8 or 93-3/8% of the $1000 par value.

We will continue with this problem, but first we want to emphasize that a bond is discounted at the market rate of interest or yield to maturity, *not* at the coupon rate (6% in the above case) stated on the bond. The coupon rate is only used to determine the future income stream that the bond will yield. What happens when the market rate of interest *changes?* Let's try it and find out:

Problem 3-12:

If the market rate of interest drops to 6½% what will happen to the market value of our bond in Problem 3-11?

Solution:

The future income stream (S_1 through S_4) is not affected since this is determined by the face amount of the bond and the coupon rate. However, we do have some new values in our present value equation, since our income stream is now discounted at 6½% instead of 8%.

$$S_0 = \frac{S_1}{(1+r)^1} + \frac{S_2}{(1+r)^2} + \cdots + \frac{S_n}{(1+r)^n}$$

$$= \frac{\$60}{(1+.065)^1} + \frac{\$60}{(1+.065)^2} + \frac{\$60}{(1+.065)^3} + \frac{\$1060}{(1+.065)^4}$$

$$= \frac{\$60}{1.0650} + \frac{\$60}{1.1342} + \frac{\$60}{1.2079} + \frac{\$1060}{1.2865}$$

$$= \$56.34 \quad + \$52.90 \quad + \$49.67 \quad + \$823.94 = \$982.85$$

The new market value of our bond is $982.85, an *increase* in value resulting from the *decrease* in the interest rate.

All we have done, of course, is to illustrate the inverse relationship between a change in the interest rate and the resulting change in the price of a bond. We illustrated this inverse relationship earlier in Figure 3-2b; this is how it looks graphically in the case of our four-year bond:

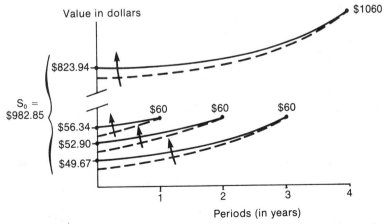

Figure 3-3. Problem 3-12: An increase in the market price of a bond caused by a reduction in the interest rate from 8% to 6½%.

As can be seen in Figure 3-3, a lower rate of interest causes the time-path of discount to rise, or become flatter, thereby resulting in a higher present value for the future cash flows. Since the market price of a bond is equal to the present value of the future cash flow, the market price of the bond increases to $982.85 from $933.76. Ever wonder why the price of a bond goes up when the interest rate falls? Now you know!

We're ready to leave the topic of bonds, but, before we do, we'd like to offer a comment on speculation in the bond market. Since the market rate of interest usually fluctuates, we can also expect the market price of a bond to vary. This is how you can speculate in nice, safe U.S. Treasury bonds: their *redemption* value is so certain that they are the standard of financial security, but their *market* value rises when interest rates fall and falls when interest rates rise.

The next problem is a little different. This time you will be asked to make a choice between two alternative future payments, one of which is an annuity.

Problem 3-13:

You are now a freshman, and your grandfather has promised you a graduation gift of $10,000 4 years from now. As an alternative you may choose to take $2000 per year until your expected graduation in 4 years. Assuming the choice is not made out of desperation, which alternative would you choose? If you decide to take the $2000 a year alternative you could invest it in 9% CDs that compound interest annually.

Solution:

The key to the problem is to compare the present value of each alternative and then choose the larger. To find the present value of the first alternative, the $10,000 payment at the end of 4 years, we simply discount for 4 periods at 9%.

$$S_0 = \frac{S_n}{(1+r)^n}$$

$$= \frac{\$10,000}{(1+.09)^4}$$

$$= \frac{\$10,000}{1.4116} = \$7084.16$$

So the first alternative has a present value of $7084.16.

To find the present value of the second alternative, which we will call S_0', we'll use the generalized present value equation (3-3):

$$S_0' = \frac{S_1}{(1+r)^1} + \frac{S_2}{(1+r)^2} + \cdots + \frac{S_n}{(1+r)^n}$$

$$= \frac{\$2000}{(1+.09)^1} + \frac{\$2000}{(1+.09)^2} + \frac{\$2000}{(1+.09)^3} + \frac{\$2000}{(1+.09)^4}$$

$$= \frac{\$2000}{1.09} + \frac{\$2000}{1.1881} + \frac{\$2000}{1.2950} + \frac{\$2000}{1.4116}$$

$$= \$1834.86 + \$1683.36 + \$1544.40 + \$1416.83 = \$6479.45.$$

So the total present value S_0', of these four separate \$2000 payments comes to \$6479.45. It looks like you'd be better off to accept \$10,000 at the end of the fourth year, since *it* has a present value of \$7084.16.

If we wanted to illustrate Problem 3-13 with a graph, it would appear as in Figure 3-4 below:

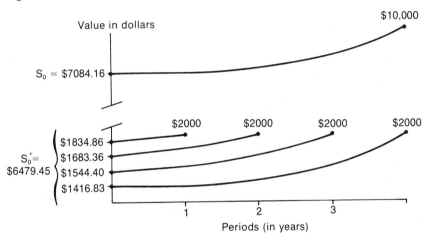

Figure 3-4. Problem 3-13: Comparing the present value of a future sum to the present value of an annuity.

This time we have two present sums on our graph. The first sum, S_0, is the present value of the \$10,000 payment in four years. The second sum, S_0', is the present value of the \$2000 annuity alternative. Since the value of S_0 is greater than the value of S_0', you would choose the \$10,000 payment at graduation.

Now for our last problem in this chapter:

Problem 3-14:

Your great-grandfather, a rich southern planter and patriot, personally financed the operations of a company of light infantry during the Civil War by establishing an 8% fund in the Bank of England in 1860. Most of 1861 was spent in training and total expenses ran to only £10,000 when bills were received for that year. In 1862, the company engaged in several battles and expenses mounted to £25,000. 1863 was even worse because of almost constant combat; during that year expenses climbed to £50,000. In 1864 it was necessary to re-equip most of the company which cost £60,000. In 1865, when hostilities ceased, £40,000 were left which went to fund a pension for the company's disabled. How much did your great-grandfather put in the fund in 1860?

Solution:

This is similar to the previous problems in that we have payments in different future time periods, although "future" in this case means future relative to 1860, when the deposit was made in the Bank of England. To find out how much this deposit was, let's work it through one year at a time.

The £10,000 paid out in 1861 could have been funded in 1860 by a deposit of

$$\frac{£10,000}{(1 + .08)^1} = \frac{£10,000}{1.08} = £9259.26.$$

The £25,000 paid out in 1862 could have been funded in 1860 by a deposit of

$$\frac{£25,000}{(1 + .08)^2} = \frac{£25,000}{1.1664} = £21,433.47.$$

The £50,000 paid out in 1863 could have been funded by a deposit of

$$\frac{£50,000}{(1 + .08)^3} = \frac{£50,000}{1.2597} = £39,691.99.$$

The £60,000 paid out in 1864 could have been funded by a deposit of

$$\frac{£60,000}{(1 + .08)^4} = \frac{£60,000}{1.3605} = £44,101.43.$$

Finally, the £40,000 left over in 1865 could have been funded by a deposit of

$$\frac{£40,000}{(1 + .08)^5} = \frac{£40,000}{1.4693} = £27,223.85.$$

Having reduced each of these future payments to their 1860 value, we add them together to get £141,710, the size of your great-grandfather's deposit.

Although we set this problem up a little differently, you should have realized that we are still using the basic format we showed you earlier in equation (3-3). Had we written the problem like this:

$$S_0 = \frac{£10,000}{(1 + .08)^1} + \frac{£25,000}{(1 + .08)^2} + \frac{£50,000}{(1 + .08)^3} + \frac{£60,000}{(1 + .08)^4} + \frac{£40,000}{(1 + .08)^5} \text{ ,}$$

we would have gotten exactly the same answer. We just worked Problem 3-14 one step at a time, but that doesn't change the nature of the problem.

SUMMARY

We've now had a look at the present value concept and, as we have seen, we were concerned with finding today's value of some future sum or sums. This is simply the reverse of the future value concept in the previous chapter where we started with a present sum and compounded it ahead to some future value. Present value problems and future value problems are basically the same except for the direction of movement along the time axis, as we illustrated earlier in Figure 3-1.

When we tried to find the present value of a single future sum, we rearranged the time value of money equation (2-8) so that the unknown variable, S_0, was set equal to the other variables for which the values were known. The resulting equation, (3-1) below, is our basic present value equation:

$$S_0 = \frac{S_n}{(1+r)^n} .$$

When we examined the case of multiple future sums, each future sum had to be discounted back to the present before it could be added. A common way to express this operation is with the expanded present value equation (3-3) below:

$$S_0 = \frac{S_1}{(1+r)^1} + \frac{S_2}{(1+r)^2} + \ . \ . \ . \ + \frac{S_n}{(1+r)^n} .$$

The case of multiple future sums is not difficult to handle, but it might be helpful to remind you of some advice we offered at the end of the last chapter: sometimes it is necessary to break a problem into its component parts before a solution can be determined. As long as you realize that any problem with three future sums can be treated as three simple problems, or any with five future sums can be treated as five simple problems, you should have no difficulty in finding the solution.

Finally, because the value of money does change over time, we need methods that will allow us to compare values of sums that exist at different points in time. The comparison can be made in the distant past, the distant future, or any year in between. However, since we always live in the *present*, it is usually convenient to make the comparison by first finding, and then comparing, the present values of these future sums.

ADDITIONAL PROBLEMS

1. What is the present value of a $236.74 sum existing 10 years from today if the discount rate is 5%?

    Answer: $145.34

2. When we worked Problem 3-13, we *could* have compounded each of the four $2000 sums ahead to year 4 for purposes of comparison rather than making the comparison in the present. If you decided to solve the problem in this manner, is your conclusion still the same?

    Answer: Yes, $9146.26, the sum of the future values, is less than the $10,000 payment in four years.

3. If a $1000 par value, 6¼% debenture from Blackout Power and Light Company pays interest annually and matures in 5 years, what is its price if it yields 8½% to maturity?

    Answer: $911.29

4. In July of 1978, you paid $95 for a 10-ounce silver ingot issued by the Benjamin Mint commemorating the July, 1969 Apollo 11 landing. The collector who sold it to you bought it when it was issued and told you that he realized a 2% annual rate of loss on this investment. What did he pay for the ingot?

    Answer: $113.94

5. You have bid successfully on a government contract for delivery of one million pounds of beef to the Food Services Depot in five years and you plan to honor the contract by raising your own herd of Black Angus. Black Angus are born roughly half bulls and half heifers and will dress out at about 1000 pounds per carcass when slaughtered a year or more later. In a growing herd, heifers are retained for breeding and bulls are sold as steers in about one year. After various factors such as fertility and mortality are taken into account, a herd of Black Angus cows (and an occasional bull) can grow about 25% annually. In 5 years you plan to slaughter the whole herd, which consists of about 75% cows and heifers and 25% steers. How many cows would you start out with now to get one million pounds of dressed beef in five years? (Hint: you only need 750,000 pounds of dressed female beef; the steers are not part of the reproductive growth cycle but are an annual product of the herd. This means that you only need to discount the 750,000 pounds back to the present and not the one million pounds.)

    Answer: 246 cows

CHAPTER 4

THE PRESENT VALUE TABLE

You probably noticed that most of the problems in the last chapter involved time periods of five years or less, a simplification intended to reduce the tedium of solving the problems. Now it's time to admit that many real problems call for discount periods of 20, 30, or 50 years and longer. In this chapter we are going to develop a table that will reduce these longer problems to more manageable proportions.

Our discussion of the present value table in this chapter is divided into several parts. In the first part we take a look at the way in which the table is constructed and used. In the second part of the chapter we'll examine some extensions of the table. For example, we'll need to know what to do when we find problems that have periods or discount rates not listed in the table. In the third part of the chapter, we'll come back to a matter we first mentioned in Chapter 2 — we'll use the present value table to solve future, as well as present, value problems. Finally, we'll take a brief look at interpolation. In short, the table can be extremely useful, but you will need to know how to extend and otherwise work with it in order to use it to its maximum advantage.

We'll begin with a discussion of the way in which a short present value table is constructed and used.

THE CONSTRUCTION AND USE OF A PRESENT VALUE TABLE

In Chapter 2, we constructed a brief future value table by computing the value of the term $(1 + r)^n$ for various interest rates and periods. We can do the same thing with our present value equation (3-1) below:

$$S_0 = \frac{S_n}{(1 + r)^n} \, .$$

But first we want to change it to

$$S_0 = S_n \times \frac{1}{(1 + r)^n},$$

so that we can define a new term, the *present value factor,* or *pvf*:

$$pvf = \frac{1}{(1 + r)^n}. \tag{4-1}$$

Having defined our factor, it should be evident that any future sum can be discounted back to the present by multiplying it by the appropriate present value factor:

$$S_0 = S_n \, (pvf). \tag{4-2}$$

Now we can construct our present value table. All we need is to find the values for the present value factor for the more commonly used periods and discount rates, and then arrange the results in a convenient table. For example, any future sum discounted for one period at 9% would be multiplied by $\frac{1}{(1 + .09)^1}$, and by $\frac{1}{(1 + .09)^2}$ if for two. Since the progression is the same for any period and any discount rate, we could construct a table of present value factors such as Table 4-1.

TABLE 4-1.   CONSTRUCTION OF A PRESENT VALUE TABLE

Periods	9%	10%	11%	12%
1	$\frac{1}{(1 + .09)^1} =$ .9174	$\frac{1}{(1 + .10)^1} =$ .9091	$\frac{1}{(1 + .11)^1} =$ .9009	$\frac{1}{(1 + .12)^1} =$ .8929
2	$\frac{1}{(1 + .09)^2} =$ .8417	$\frac{1}{(1 + .10)^2} =$ .8264	$\frac{1}{(1 + .11)^2} =$ .8116	$\frac{1}{(1 + .12)^2} =$ .7972
3	$\frac{1}{(1 + .09)^3} =$ .7722	$\frac{1}{(1 + .10)^3} =$ .7513	$\frac{1}{(1 + .11)^3} =$ .7312	$\frac{1}{(1 + .12)^3} =$ .7118
4	$\frac{1}{(1 + .09)^4} =$ .7084	$\frac{1}{(1 + .10)^4} =$ .6830	$\frac{1}{(1 + .11)^4} =$ .6587	$\frac{1}{(1 + .12)^4} =$ .6355
5	$\frac{1}{(1 + .09)^5} =$ .6499	$\frac{1}{(1 + .10)^5} =$ .6209	$\frac{1}{(1 + .11)^5} =$ .5935	$\frac{1}{(1 + .12)^5} =$ .5674

Even the construction of a longer present value table is a relatively simple matter as the next problem illustrates:

Problem 4-1:

Can you use your electronic calculator to construct a present value table for periods 1 through 10 using a 9% discount rate?

Solution:

Of course! First we'll write the equation for the present value factor,

$$\frac{1}{(1 + r)^n},$$

and then we'll execute the following steps:

Arithmetic	**Algebraic**
1. set for floating decimal	1. enter numerator "1"
2. constant key on	2. press ÷ key
3. enter the numerator "1"	3. enter 1.09 (for 1 + 9%)
4. press the ÷ key	4. press the = key and record the answer for the first period (.9174 appears in the display)
5. enter 1.09 (for 1 + 9%)	
6. press the ± key and record the answer for the first period (.9174 appears in the display)	5. press the = key again and record the answer for the second period
7. press the ± key again and record the answer for the second period	6. continue to press the = key until you have found and recorded the present value factors for each of the ten periods.
8. continue to press the ± key until you have found and recorded the present value factors for each of the ten periods.	

Note that we did not try to use the calculator with the exponential key in this problem. Unless the algebraic calculator with the exponential key has a built-in constant feature, and many do not, you must calculate each value separately.

If you worked the problem correctly, you should have found a factor of .4224 in the tenth period. With this factor in hand, we can easily find the present value of our $236.74 inheritance of the previous chapter by using expression (4-2) above:

$$S_0 = S_n \, (pvf)$$

$$= \$236.74(.4224) = \$100.$$

This is the same answer we derived earlier. By the way, if your calculator does have a constant feature, substitute $236.74 in place of the "1" (the numerator in the present value factor equation) in Problem 4-1 above and repeat the steps. The answer that appears in the display when you press the equals key the tenth time should be $100.

Now let's try another problem using the factors in our present value table:

Problem 4-2:

In 1970 Banco Nacional de Mexico was selling 1000 peso deposit certificates yielding 12% interest compounded annually after Mexican taxes. If you knew that in 1974 you would need 157,356 pesos to pay for a small cottage you were having built on your leasehold property on the beach at Zihuatanejo, how many 1000 peso certificates would you have had to purchase in 1970?

Solution:

Remember that a present value problem is simply a compound interest problem worked backward. Rephrased, the question is: what sum compounded at 12% will grow to 157,356 in 4 years? Simple: the 157,356 pesos is the future value so we just multiply it by the present value factor for 4 periods at 12% (which can be found in Table 4-1 or in the longer table in the Appendix) to get

$$S_0 = S_n \text{ (pvf)}$$

$$= 157,356(.6355) = 100,000 \text{ pesos.}$$

You would have had to purchase 100 certificates in 1000 peso denominations in 1970.

P.S. If you really want to *own* coastal property in Mexico, get a good lawyer. It's illegal for foreigners.

Now let's use the longer present value table in the Appendix to give you a chance to become familiar with it:

Problem 4-3:

In our banana export problem of the last chapter (Problem 3-3), we found the present value of a $5,000,000 sum 3 years in the future by using the present value equation. Try it again using the present value table in the Appendix. (The discount rate for the problem is 4%.)

Solution:

Well, you have to have $5,000,000 3 years from now and your account earns 4%, so we look in the table for 3 periods at 4% and find the .8890 factor. We simply multiply this factor times $5,000,000 to find our present value:

$$S_0 = S_n \text{ (pvf)}$$

$$= \$5,000,000(.8890) = \$4,445,000.$$

In order to have $5,000,000 in 3 years, you must start with $4,445,000. (This is $160.46 more than we obtained in Problem 3-3 and it's about $18 larger than the answer we would get if we found the pvf with our calculator. The difference in each case is simply due to rounding.)

In cases where interest is compounded semiannually, quarterly, or even monthly, the present value table can be used if a discount rate corresponding to the rate used for the discount period can be found.

Problem 4-4:

If your savings account has a $106.14 balance today, how large was the single deposit you made one year ago if the account pays 6% stated annual interest compounded quarterly?

Solution:

This problem is really no different from earlier ones (such as Problem 3-8) in which interest is compounded other than yearly. Since the discount rate per period is $\frac{6\%}{4}$ or 1.5%, and since the number of time periods is 4, we could look in the present value table under the 1.5% column and along the 4th period row to find the present value factor of .9422. Once we multiply this times our future sum, we'll have our answer:

$$S_0 = S_n \text{(pvf)}$$

$$= \$106.14(.9422) = \$100.$$

Remember that we are always concerned with the interest per *period*. For example, if the interest was paid semiannually, we would have looked in the second period row under the $\frac{6\%}{2}$ or 3% column. Likewise, if the interest had been compounded monthly, we would look under the $\frac{6\%}{12}$ or .5% column to find the appropriate present value factor.

By the way, notice that if the stated annual interest rate had been 5¼%, instead of 6%, we wouldn't have been able to use the table since we don't have columns for $\frac{5¼\%}{4}$ or 1.3125%. If this had been the case, we would have had to resort to our calculator and construct a factor for 1.3125% at 4 periods. Sometimes, however, you will find extensive present value tables that have values for rates as low as 1/4%, 1/3%, 1/2% and so on—rates that at first would seem to be useless in a world where the actual interest rate is closer to 8%, 10%, or 12%. The low rates can be used in cases where the stated annual rate is compounded or discounted on a basis other than annual. Even so, extensive tables seldom have the exact rate you need, so it's a good idea to know how to use your calculator to find the factor algebraically.

The real value of the table becomes apparent when the problem concerns multiple sums in the future, each of which must be discounted before they can be added. We're going to try a problem we've already worked in the previous chapter, but this time we want to use our table and change the format of the solution.

Problem 4-5:

If your great-grandfather was able to obtain a 9%, instead of an 8%, account in the Bank of England for his £141,710 deposit back in 1860 (Problem 3-14), how much was left in the pension fund in 1865?

Solution:

The first step is to find the present (1860) value of the expenditures in years 1861 through 1864. This amount can then be subtracted from the initial deposit to find the 1860 value of the funds available for the pension fund five years later.

To find the 1860 value of the expenditures, we'll multiply each future payment by the appropriate present value factor and then add the present values. Since several future sums are involved, we'll use the following format to save a little space:

Year	Expenditure	pvf at 9%	Present (1860) Value of Expenditure
1861	£10,000	.9174	£ 9,174
1862	£25,000	.8417	£21,043
1863	£50,000	.7722	£38,610
1864	£60,000	.7084	£42,504
			£111,331

So the 1860 value of the expenditures amounted to £111,331, leaving £30,379 available for the pension fund. But we don't want its value in 1860, we want it in 1865. What do we do?

Simple: Go back and use the future value equation (2-8):

$$S_n = S_0(1 + r)^n$$

$$= £30,379(1 + .09)^5$$

$$= £30,379(1.5386) = £46,741.$$

Now we have the value of the money left over in 1865.

So much for the present value table. You've seen how it is constructed, you know where to find it and you know how to use it. Let's go now to some of the extensions we mentioned in the introduction to the chapter.

EXTENDING THE PRESENT VALUE TABLE

A present value table can be used to shorten some of the computation, but what do you do when the table doesn't have enough periods or enough discount rates? In the case of too few periods, it turns out that the table can still be of use as we shall see in the next problem.

Problem 4-6:

Your son was born today and you want to arrange a $5000 gift for him when he retires at age 60. How much do you put in a 5% savings account today if the interest is compounded annually?

Solution:

First, turn to the present value table to find the factor for 60 years at 5%. What did you find? The table stops at 50 years, right? Too bad. (Stop and think about it a little, or admit defeat and read on.)

Well, if one 60-year period is only two 30-year periods, we could take a thirty-period factor for 5% and find the value of the gift 30 years from now:

$$S_{30} = S_{60} \text{ (pvf)}$$

$$= \$5000(.2314) \quad = \$1157.00.$$

But what is its worth today? Simple: discount it another 30 years:

$$S_0 = S_{30} \text{ (pvf)}$$

$$= \$1157.00(.2314) = \$267.73.$$

If we use a 5% discount rate, $5000 60 years from now is worth $267.73 today.

It might be easier to visualize the 60-year problem if we illustrate it in Figure 4-1, in which the last 30 years are represented by the solid line and the first 30 years by the dotted line. This is similar to those problems we warned you about in Chapter 2: in order to solve the problem, it first has to be broken down into its component parts.

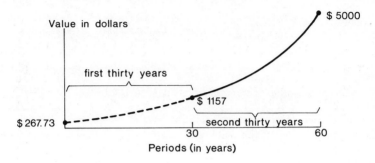

Figure 4-1.   Problem 4-6: Converting a 60-year discount period into two 30-year periods.

Of course, 60 years is not just two 30-year periods. It is also three 20-year periods, six 10-years periods, or a 5-, a 40-, and a 15-year period. Any of these combinations will give us a discount factor which will yield the same answer.

For example, we could have multiplied the two 30-year factors together to get

$$S_0 = \$5000(.2314)\,(.2314)$$
$$= \$5000(.2314)^2$$
$$= \$5000(.0535) = \$267.50.$$

Or, had we used three 20-year periods, we could have written the problem as

$$S_0 = \$5000(.3769)^3$$
$$= \$5000(.0535) = \$267.50,$$

where .3769 is the present value factor at 20 years, 5%. Or, we could have even used a 5-, a 40- and a 15-year period:

$$S_0 = \$5000(.7835)\,(.1420)\,(.4810)$$
$$= \$5000(.0535) = \$267.50.$$

The answer is the same in each case, although slight variations are possible due to rounding. Here's another one:

Problem 4-7:

In 1626, Manhattan Island was purchased from the Indians for a mere $24 worth of trinkets. Three hundred and fifty years later the island, less improvements, had a value of fifteen billion dollars ($15,000,000,000.) If the Dutch settlers instead had had the option of depositing the $24 in a 6% account in the Bank of Amsterdam, and if their heirs had moved the deposit to the Bank of England in 1819 when the Amsterdam bank wound up its affairs, who got the best of the deal, the Indians or the settlers?

Solution:

How much is fifteen billion dollars in 1976 worth in 1626, more or less than $24? Well, 350 years is only 7 50-year periods, so we find the 50 period, 6% factor (which is .0543) and solve the problem.

$$S_0 = \$15,000,000,000(.0543)^7$$

$$= \$15,000,000,000(.00000000139) = \$20.85$$

How about that! The crafty Dutch paid too much.

As you can see, any present value table with 50 periods is usually long enough. Perhaps a more common problem is that the table won't have enough discount rates. What do you do then?

You could interpolate, which is a way of estimating a given discount rate from rates that are already available in the tables, or you could go to your calculator and work it out algebraically. However, we do want to spend a little time on interpolation, so we've saved it for later in the chapter. Instead, let's work a problem with our calculator to find a factor that isn't in the table.

Problem 4-8:

For some time now, you've been saving your money for a return visit to Mt. Katadin in Baxter State Park. Since this will involve a bit of a drive, let alone a climb, you figure that you will need exactly $1000 next year when you go. After shopping around, you've decided that the best way to get the most interest on the money you've already saved is to purchase a one-year CD at your local savings and loan association, which pays 6½% interest compounded semiannually. How much do you need today if you want to purchase one of these CDs so that your trip will be fully funded?

Solution:

The problem involves two periods with a discount rate of $\frac{6\frac{1}{2}\%}{2}$ or 3.25%.
You don't have a column for 3.25% in your table, but you do know how to write the formula for the present value factor:

$$\text{pvf} \;=\; \frac{1}{(1 + r)^n}$$

$$=\; \frac{1}{(1 + .0325)^2} \;=\; .9380.$$

If you multiply this by the $1000 future sum, you'll need $938 today.

We didn't bother to show the calculator steps in this problem; we've already done it in Problem 4-1. In fact, you'll soon discover (if you haven't done so already) that it's usually quicker to reach for your calculator rather than the table when you need to find a present value factor. You'll need the calculator anyway when it comes to finishing the problem, so why not figure the factor on the calculator while you're at it?

FINDING FUTURE VALUES

Now that we've dealt with some extensions to the present value table, let's turn to yet another application: we want to use our *present* value table to solve *future* value problems like those we solved in Chapter 2. Perhaps the best place to start is with a comparison of Tables 2-1 and 4-1, on pages 17 and 42, respectively.

Recall that we constructed Table 2-1 by finding the numerical equivalent for $(1 + r)^n$ for various interest rates and time periods, while in Table 4-1 we solved for $\frac{1}{(1 + r)^n}$. Since one is the reciprocal of the other we can express the relationship between the two factors as follows:

$$\text{fvf} = \frac{1}{\text{pvf}} \cdot \qquad (4\text{-}3)$$

If a future value factor is just the reciprocal of the present value factor, then any operation that can be done with a future value table can be done with a present value table instead.

Problem 4-9:

In Problem 2-1, we found the future value of a $100 deposit left in the bank for 10 years at 9% compounded annually. Rework the problem using the present value table rather than the future value formula.

Solution:

Instead of multiplying the present $100 sum times the future value factor, we divide it by the present value factor for 10 periods at 9% (or .4224), which is the same thing.

$$S_{10} = \frac{S_0}{pvf}$$

$$= \frac{\$100}{.4224} = \$236.74$$

Again, this is exactly the same answer we obtained earlier, since dividing $100 by .4224 is the same as multiplying it by 2.3674.

When we worked future value problems in Chapter 2, we multiplied the present sum by the appropriate future value factor in Table 2-1. This time we divided the present sum by the present value factor in Table 4-1. It's the same thing since the two factors are reciprocals, a point worth emphasizing:

In any operation that calls for multiplication by one of these factors, the same result can be obtained by dividing by the other factor instead.

This rule is so simple, you can see why it is unnecessary to have *both* a future and a present value table; either one will do. Now we'll try another problem.

Problem 4-10:

Go back to the Civil War financing problem (4-5), and use the present value table to find the 1865 value of the disabled veterans' pension fund, which was worth £30,379 in 1860.

Solution:

To find the 1865 future value, all we have to do is divide the present sum by the present value factor for 9%, 5 periods that we found in Table 4-1:

$$S_n = \frac{S_0}{pvf}$$

$$= \frac{£30,379}{pvf}$$

$$= \frac{£30,379}{.6499} = £46,744.$$

At the end of the war, there would have been £46,744 left in the pension fund.

By the way, sometimes you might become confused about when to multiply and when to divide. No problem: since the present value *must* be smaller than the future value for all *positive* rates of return, do the operation (multiplication or division) that makes it come out that way.

AN INTRODUCTION TO INTERPOLATION

Now that we've examined some additional uses of the present value table, we come to the last topic in this chapter, a brief introduction to interpolation. For the most part, interpolation is a relatively simple technique and will be used rather extensively in the next chapter. Right now, however, we want to try a little problem and see if we can learn anything from it.

Problem 4-11:

Suppose we don't have the table in the back of the book, and yet we want the present value factor for 6% at 3 periods. We do happen to have the third period values for 4% and 8%, and we know that 6% is exactly halfway in between. What do we do?

Solution:

Since 6% is halfway between 4% and 8%, we could try to find the factor that is halfway between the 4% factor and the 8% factor:

$$
\begin{array}{rl}
\text{pvf for 8\% in period 3} = & .7938 \\
\text{pvf for 4\% in period 3} = & \underline{.8890} \\
& 1.6828 \div 2 = .8414.
\end{array}
$$

So, .8414 is halfway between .7938 and .8890 and is the *interpolated* present value factor for 6%. To check this number let's compute it:

$$
\frac{1}{(1 + .06)^3} = .8396.
$$

It didn't work! That's more error than we can attribute to rounding off numbers.

We can, however, explain why we didn't get the correct answer with the aid of Figure 4-2. In this figure we have plotted the present value factors for several discount rates for periods 1 through 4. Inspection of the graph reveals that the solid lines connecting the present value factors for each discount rate become closer together as the discount rate goes higher.

Point A on the figure is the present value factor for 4% in the third period and has a value of .8890. Likewise, point C is the factor for 8% in the same period and has a value of .7938. In Problem 4-11 we tried to average these values in an effort to estimate point B (which has a value of .8396), but failed to get the correct answer. Now you can see why: point B is *not* halfway between points A and C.

If we tried to estimate point B by averaging the values at E (.9423) and D (.7513), we would have an answer of .8468, which is even worse than our first try. Again the reason for the error is that point B is not halfway between these points. We'll do more interpolation in the next chapter, but when we do we'll always interpolate over the smallest possible range in order to minimize the error.

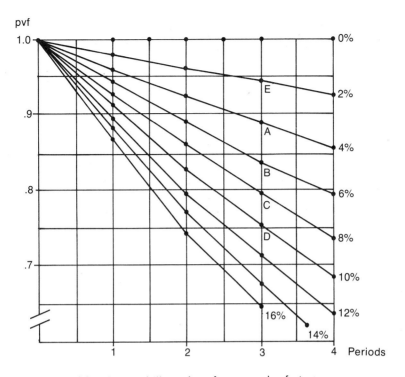

Figure 4-2. Graphical illustration of present value factors.

SUMMARY

In this chapter, we dealt with the construction and use of the present value table. First we defined a new term, our present value factor, and then showed how a future sum could be discounted back to the present by multiplying it times this factor:

$$S_0 = S_n(\text{pvf}).$$

The values for these factors can be computed with a calculator as they are needed, or, for convenience, they can be computed for various values of n and r and then be arranged in a table as in Table 4-1.

A table is convenient to have, but we also realize that a table won't always have the exact number of periods or the discount rate that we need. Whenever the problem is that of not enough periods, we simply take the product of two (or more) present value factors in order to find the factor for the longer period. If the table does not have enough discount rates, we can find them with our calculator, or we can interpolate.

When it comes to working future value problems, we observed that the future value factor is the reciprocal of the present value factor:

$$\text{fvf} = \frac{1}{\text{pvf}}.$$

Because one is the inverse of the other, it is not necessary to have *both* future and present value tables; either table can be used to solve present, as well as future, value problems.

In the last part of the chapter, we took a brief look at interpolation. We'll be doing more interpolation in the next chapter, but for now you should realize that this method always involves some error. In fact, one of the best ways to find a present value factor is with your pocket or desk calculator. Since you'll usually need the calculator to finish the problem, it will save time if you know how to compute the factor so that you won't have to reach for your table.

We're ready for a new chapter and a new topic, but first we want to leave you with a word of caution. A present value table can simplify many problems, but don't lose sight of the process involved. All too often individuals can solve problems using the table without fully understanding what is being done. Because of this we purposely delayed explaining the construction and use of the table until this chapter; it is simply more important to fully understand the time value concept before the short cuts are revealed.

ADDITIONAL PROBLEMS

1. What is the present value factor for 8.98% at 10 periods? (Hint: you need the calculator for this one.)

   Answer: .4232

2. What is the present value factor for a discount rate of −7.5% in the fourth period?

   Answer: 1.3659

3. What discount rate will *always* equate the value of S_n to S_0, regardless of the number of years separating the two sums?

   Answer: a 0% discount rate

4. If you have exactly $546.93 in your account today and you wanted to know its value exactly one year ago, what present value factor would you use if the 4% stated annual interest had been compounded quarterly?

   Answer: .9610

5. The Euphorian tribe of the Euthanasian Islands sets aside a fund at birth to finance the newborn's eventual funeral and ceremonial expenses. According to tradition, a first class ceremony (for a chief or heir apparent only) costs 30,000 cowrie shells and the life expectancy for male members of the royal family is 70 years. How many cowrie shells should be deposited with the tribal treasurer (who at the end of each year pays in one cowrie shell for each ten on deposit) to fully fund the funeral expenses of the Chief's first son, born this year?

    Answer: 38 cowrie shells

6. The Last National Bank in your hometown is trying to attract additional deposits by compounding and paying interest *daily*. You have a modest $100 deposit in another bank which pays the same interest (5% on regular passbook accounts), but compounds the interest quarterly. How much larger would your account be at the end of one year if you switched banks in order to take advantage of the daily compounding? (Hint: set your calculator for floating decimal and use a 360-day year.)

    Answer: $0.3

CHAPTER 5

THE DISCOUNTED RATE OF RETURN

When we began the time value of money topic, we developed a simple equation with four unknowns: S_n, S_0, r, and n. In Chapter 2 we dealt with problems in which the first of these variables, S_n, was the unknown to be found. In Chapters 3 and 4 we worked problems when S_0 was the only unknown. In this chapter we will analyze a third type of time value problem in which r, the discount rate, is the unknown term, while the remaining variables S_n, S_0, and n are known. In other words, we want to find the discount (or interest) rate that will make the *present value* of a given future payment equal to a given payment today.

In the case of a single future sum, we can solve for the discount rate in two ways: we can use the time value equation and solve algebraically, or we can use the present value tables developed in the last chapter and search for the rate among those listed. When more than one future sum is involved, however, the discount rate that makes these future sums equal in value to a given present sum must be found by trial and error.

Let's begin our discussion of the discounted rate of return by examining the case of a single future sum.

THE DISCOUNTED RATE OF RETURN WITH A SINGLE FUTURE SUM

Using the Algebraic Solution. In previous chapters, we began with a discussion of the time value of money equation and then rearranged it so that the unknown term was set equal to the known terms in the expression. We'll do the same thing in this chapter, only this time we'll solve for the discount rate, r.

First, we begin with our time value of money equation (2-8):

$$S_n = S_0 (1 + r)^n.$$

By dividing both sides by S_0, we get

$$(1 + r)^n = \frac{S_n}{S_0},$$

and by taking the n*th* root of each side we have

$$1 + r = \sqrt[n]{\frac{S_n}{S_0}}$$

Finally, we subtract 1 from both sides to get the *discount rate of return equation*:

$$r = \sqrt[n]{\frac{S_n}{S_0}} - 1. \qquad (5\text{-}1)$$

Now we have it! The question is, can we use it? Let's go to a problem and find out.

Problem 5-1:

Ten years ago you bought shares of General Consolidated Industries at $100 and after a 10-year record of no dividend payments, you want to sell. If you net $236.74 after selling the stock, what was the annual rate of return on your investment?

Solution:

We have the present value ($100), the future value ($236.74), and the number of periods (10), so we should be able to use the discount rate of return equation (5-1) to find the value for r:

$$r = \sqrt{\frac{S_n}{S_0}} - 1$$

$$= \sqrt[10]{\frac{236.74}{100}} - 1 = \sqrt[10]{2.3674} - 1.$$

Now we have another problem: how do we find the 10th root of 2.3674? Well, if your calculator is equipped with an exponential power key, the answer is relatively simple. Since the n*th* root of a number is that number raised to the $\frac{1}{n}$ power, we would complete the problem as follows:

$$r = 2.3674^{\frac{1}{10}} - 1$$

$$= 2.3674^{.1} - 1$$

$$= 1.0900 \quad - 1 = .09.$$

The discount rate, r, is equal to .09, or 9%.

Obviously the $\boxed{\sqrt[y]{x}}$ power key is a useful feature. If your calculator has one, you should be able to find the nth root of any number. As for the discount rate, we have now found a value for r that can be used to discount the future sum of $236.74 back to a present value of $100. (It is also the interest rate that could be used to compound a present sum of $100 for 10 periods until it reached a future value of $236.74.) Now that you've got the idea, let's try another.

Problem 5-2:

Fourteen years ago, 2 baseball card collectors paid $.40 for a 1910 Honus Wagner card showing Mr. Wagner on the reverse side of a cigarette advertisement. If they expect to sell the card for $3000 next year at the International Bubble Gum Card Collectors Convention, what would be the annual rate of return on their initial $.40 investment?

Solution:

First we write the discount rate of return equation (5-1) below:

$$r = \sqrt[n]{\frac{S_n}{S_0}} \quad -1.$$

Then, with S_n = $3000, n = 15, and S_0 = $.40, we fill in the values to get

$$r = \sqrt[15]{\frac{3000}{.40}} - 1$$

$$= \sqrt[15]{7500} - 1$$

$$= 7500^{.0667} - 1 = 1.8133 - 1 = .8133$$

or 81.33%, which is not a bad rate of return on any investment.

Speaking of rates of return on investment, bear in mind that you won't always make out so well. For example, let's look at the commodity futures market in *Brassica napus*:

Problem 5-3:

Six months ago you got a $1000 birthday bonus which you immediately put to use as a stake in your scheme to make an immodest fortune in the commodities market. The $1000 was deposited with your broker as security on your contract to sell 5000 bushels of number 1 Canadian rapeseed at $3.10 per bushel for delivery in Thunder Bay, Ontario, the following December (today). Not only have you never owned the 5000 bushels that you have contracted to sell, but you would not know a rapeseed if you were accosted by one. If rapeseed sells for $3.22 per bushel in December (when your contract calls for delivery), what monthly discounted rate of return did you get on your investment?

Solution:

Let's see, when you sell you'll receive 5000 bushels times $3.10, which amounts to $15,500! Pretty good haul for only a $1000 investment. Of course, before you can sell 5000 bushels of rapeseed you have to *own* 5000 bushels. To do that you have to *buy* 5000 bushels at $3.22 a bushel (gulp!). Five thousand bushels times $3.22 equals $16,100, so that $15,500 revenue minus the $16,100 cost gives you a loss of $600! That leaves you with only $400 of your original $1000 investment, obviously a negative rate of return on investment.

$$r = \sqrt[6]{\frac{400}{1000}} \quad -1$$

$$= \sqrt[6]{.4} \quad -1$$

$$= .4^{.1667} \quad -1 = .8583 - 1 = -14.17\%$$

So, a −14.17% monthly discount rate makes $400 today equivalent to $1000 six months ago. Appropriate for your plunge into the rapeseed market, don't you think?

In the above problem, we were able to use the discount rate of return equation to find a *negative* discount rate. We'll be using the present value table in a moment to solve similar types of problems, but since the table doesn't have negative discount rates, the algebraic approach to the solution does have its advantages.

Using the Present Value Table. Our second method of finding the discount rate when the problem involves a single future sum involves the use of the present value table. This time, we're simply going to turn to our table and search for the discount rate using the known values for the remaining variables. In order to see how this can be done, let's review some material discussed earlier.

In Chapter 4, we discovered that the present value table simplified some of the work because some of the computation is done for you. In fact, we found that we could discount any future sum to its present value by simply multiplying the future sum by the present value factor, an operation we summarized in expression (4-2) below:

$$S_0 = S_n \text{ (pvf)}.$$

Of course, we could divide both sides by S_n to get

$$pvf \ = \ \frac{S_0}{S_n},$$

(5-2)

and this is where we will start, with the observation that

Any present value factor represents the ratio of the present sum to the future sum.

In order to show how this can be of use to us, we'll use it in a problem we just worked:

Problem 5-4:

In the first problem in this chapter, we asked for the rate of return on your investment if you sold your shares of General Consolidated Industries for $236.74 after having bought them 10 years ago for $100. Can you find the rate of return with the present value table in the Appendix?

Solution:

With a present value of $100 and a future value of $236.74, we can use expression (5-2) to find the present value factor.

$$pvf \ = \ \frac{S_0}{S_n}$$

$$= \ \frac{\$100}{\$236.74} \ = \ .4224$$

Now we simply search for this factor in the table along the 10th period row and note the discount rate under which it is found. If you run your finger across the factors in this row, you will find .4224 in the 9% column. You get a 9% rate of return on your investment.

Not all problems work out with a factor that can be found in the table. Usually we have to interpolate. What would we do if our table were set up without a 9% column and instead had discount rates for only 6, 8, 10% and so on? We would again look across the 10th period row until we found two values, the first greater and the second smaller than .4224. We would soon discover that our discount rate was between 8% (which has a present value factor of .4632) and 10% (which has a present value factor of .3855). Let's interpolate to see how it's done. If we discounted the future sum of $236.74 at 10%, we would have

$$\$236.74(.3855) \ = \ \$91.26,$$

and if we discounted at 8%, we would have

$$\$236.74(.4632) = \$109.66.$$

Since the present value discounted at 10% is less than $100 and the present value discounted at 8% is more, we know that there must be some discount rate, r, between 8% and 10%, that will equate the $100 present sum with the $236.74 future payment. To find that particular discount rate, we'll interpolate using the following format:

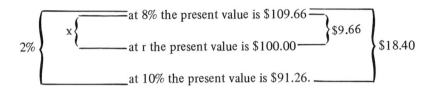

Then

$$\frac{x}{2\%} = \frac{\$\ 9.66}{\$18.40}$$

$$\frac{x}{2\%} = .5250$$

$$x = (.5250)(2\%) = 1.05\%.$$

Since we must add 1.05% to our lower bracket (8%), we now have

$$r = 8\% + x$$

$$= 8\% + 1.05\% = 9.05\%.$$

In other words, we know that at 8% the present value of $236.74 is $109.66 and at 10% it is $91.26. We also know that there is some discount rate, r, that will discount $236.74 back to $100. By letting the distance between 8% and r equal some value, x, we set up a proportion and find that x has a value of 1.05%. Adding this to 8%, we found the value of r to be 9.05%.* This is close to the 9% we already know to be correct. Let's verify our answer:

---

*Of course, we could have let the distance between 10% and r be our value for x and then set up the proportion like this:

$$\frac{x}{2\%} = \frac{\$8.74}{\$18.40}.$$

The value for x in this case would be .95% which, when *subtracted* from 10%, would leave us with r = 9.05%. Although the proportion can be set up either way, we'll continue to interpolate from the lower discount rate as we have done in the text above.

Problem 5-5:

Use your calculator to check the interpolation results just derived above.

Solution:

Since we are discounting $236.74 by 9.05%, we'll proceed as follows:

Arithmetic	Algebraic
1. set for floating decimal	1. enter $236.74
2. constant key on	2. press $\div$ key
3. enter $236.74	3. enter 1.0905
4. press $\div$ key	4. press $=$ key *ten* times,
5. enter 1.0905	or:
6. press $\frac{+}{=}$ key *ten* times	1. enter "1"
	2. press $\div$ key
	3. enter 1.0905
	4. press $\boxed{y^x}$ key
	5. enter 10
	6. press $=$ key
	7. press $\boxed{x}$ key
	8. enter $236.74
	9. press $=$ key.

We got $99.54, which is not quite the $100 we expected. The $.46 error is due to interpolation over a 2% spread. If we had been able to interpolate over a narrower range, say between 8.5% and 9.5%, our value for r would have been closer to the exact answer of 9%.

As we shall see in the next problem, the rate of return on investment can be found anytime we know the initial outlay, the time period, and the final sum.

Problem 5-6:

In 1975, a well-known coin company in southern Florida offered a $5, 1953B series silver certificate in uncirculated condition for $10. If the coin company obtained this bill at the bank in 1957 (the bill carried the 1953 date until early 1957 when the date was changed), held it in a safe-deposit box until it had some value to collectors, and finally sold it 18 years later in 1975 for $10, what would be the rate of return on the initial $5 investment?

Solution:

First we find the ratio of present value to future value (that is, we find the present value factor):

$$\text{pvf} = \frac{S_0}{S_n}$$

$$= \frac{\$5}{\$10} = .5000.$$

Then we look in the present value tables in the 18th period row to discover that our discount rate is between 3.5% (.5384) and 4.0% (.4936). The present value of $10 at each discount rate is

$$S_0 \text{ at } 3.5\% = \$10(.5384) = \$5.38$$

$$S_0 \text{ at } 4.0\% = \$10(.4936) = \$4.94$$

Then, by interpolating, we find the value of r:

.5% { x { at 3.5% the present value is $5.38 } $.38 } $.44
       at r the present value is $5.00
       at 4% the present value is $4.94,

$$\frac{x}{.5\%} = \frac{\$.38}{\$.44} \qquad = .8636$$

$$x = .8636(.5\%) = .43\%,$$

and

$$r = 3.5\% + x$$

$$= 3.5\% + .43\% = 3.93\%.$$

The rate of return on investment appears to be 3.93%; it is the discount rate that equates $10 in the future with $5 in the present. We should check this by discounting the $10 back to the present using our present value equation:

$$S_0 = \frac{S_n}{(1+r)^n}$$

$$= \frac{\$10}{(1+.0393)^{18}}$$

$$= \frac{\$10}{2.0014} = \$4.997.$$

Pretty close: the error is less than ½ cent. We therefore conclude that 3.93% is close enough to the rate of return on investment for this problem. (There is no reason why you couldn't use the method described in Problem 5-5 either, just divide $10 by 1.0393 eighteen times using the $\boxed{=}$ key and you get the same answer.

By the way, you should have noticed that the interpolation took place over a .5% interval instead of the 2% interval used earlier. Although any interval can be used, we want to remind you of something we warned you about at the close of the last chapter:

In order to minimize the error, interpolate over the smallest range possible.

Our next problem is similar to the one above and is included to give you a little more practice with interpolation.

Problem 5-7:

This morning you paid $50 for a rare edition of a Superman comic that you have already contracted to sell to another collector in 10 years for $190. What will be your rate of return on your $50 investment? (In other words, what discount rate will make the $50 you paid today equivalent to the $190 you will receive in 10 years?)

Solution:

First we compute our present value factor:

$$\text{pvf} = \frac{S_0}{S_n}$$

$$= \frac{\$50}{\$190} = .2632,$$

and then turn to the 10th period row in our tables to discover that the .2632 factor lies between the 14% and the 14½% discount rates (.2697 and .2582 respectively).

We then find the present value of $190 at each discount rate:

$$S_0 \text{ at } 14\% = \$190(.2697) = \$51.24$$

$$S_0 \text{ at } 14.5\% = \$190(.2582) = \$49.06,$$

and then interpolate:

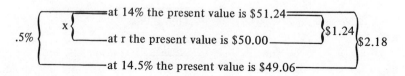

$$\frac{x}{.5\%} = \frac{\$1.24}{\$2.18}$$

$$x = .5688(.5\%) = .28\%,$$

and

$$r = 14.0\% + x$$

$$= 14.0\% + .28\% = 14.28\%.$$

Again, it's good practice to check our results, so we'll proceed as follows:

$$S_0 = \frac{S_n}{(1+r)^n}$$

$$= \frac{\$190}{(1+.1428)^{10}}$$

$$= \frac{\$190}{(3.7993)} = \$50.01.$$

So the rate of return in this problem is 14.28%.

We don't want to forget how to solve problems involving interest compounded daily, quarterly, or semiannually, so let's try this one:

Problem 5-8:

When you were 10 years old, your father put $500 in a bank account for your unrestricted use when you came of age. Now that you are 21, your little deposit has a current worth of $962.65. If the interest was compounded quarterly, what was the true or effective annual rate of return on the account?

Solution:

The deposit may have been compounded 44 times over the 11-year period, but it's the 11-year period that concerns us since we want to find the annual rate of return. First we find the present value factor with the use of expression (5-2):

$$Pvf = \frac{S_0}{S_n} = \frac{\$500}{\$962.65} = .5194.$$

Next we go to the table and look across the 11th period row until we find .5194 between the .5268 factor in the 6% column and the .5002 factor in the 6.5% column. If you care to interpolate, this will yield a rate of return of 6.14% on an annual basis.

If you wanted to find the *quarterly* rate of return, simply look for the .5194 factor in the 44th period row where it can be found in the 1.5% column (the account in this particular problem payed 6% stated annual interest compounded quarterly, or 1.5% each quarter).

Whenever we work with problems in which the stated annual interest rate is compounded daily, monthly, quarterly, or semiannually, remember that the actual or true rate of return on an annual basis will always be larger than the stated annual rate. For example, if the stated annual interest of 6% is compounded monthly, any sum deposited for one year would have a value in twelve months of:

$$S_n = S_0(1 + \frac{6\%}{12})^{12}$$

$$= S_0(1.005)^{12} = S_0(1.0617).$$

Or, the value of the future sum would be 6.17% larger at the end of the year. The stated annual interest rate may be 6%, but the true yield is higher.

If you've been wondering where we came up with these odd problems, we'll let you in on a little secret — many of them come from the real world. In fact, it's almost impossible to dream up problems stranger than some we run across in our own hometowns.

Problem 5-9:

In 1975 a prominent local bank offered an "instant interest" certificate of deposit in an attempt to evade Regulation Q limits on maximum rates of interest paid on small certificates. *All interest that would accrue during the life of the certificate was paid at the time it was purchased*, hence the term "instant interest." The highest rate available was 7½% and the longest maturity was 6 years. Since the instant interest provision in effect lowers the purchase cost of the CD, what would be the rate of return on your investment if you bought one of these 7½%, 6-year CDs?

Solution:

According to this novel plan, an investor would earn $75 interest on $1000 for each of the six years for a total interest of $75 times 6, or $450. Since this interest is paid in advance, the *initial* net cost of the CD is $1000 less $450 or $550. Of course you receive no more interest payments since it's been paid out already, but you do get your $1000 back in six years at maturity (essentially a six-year discount note). Using expression (5-2), we start by computing the present value factor:

$$pvf = \frac{S_0}{S_n}$$

$$= \frac{\$550}{\$1000} = .5500.$$

Looking across the 6th period row, we find that the rate of return is almost 10½%, *not* 7½%. (If you want to practice your interpolation, you should get an answer of 10.48%.)

Notice that the total payments would be the same as a normal 7½%, 6-year certificate of deposit: $1000 paid in and $1450 paid back. The only difference is the time at which the payments are made. The difference in yields is due to the payment of the $450 interest immediately rather than at the end of each of the 6 years. If the bank had offered a 7½%, 10-year certificate, $750 would be paid back on the purchase of a $1000 certificate all for a net initial cost of only $250. Looking in the present value table along the 10th period row for $250/$1,000 (or .2500), we find that the yield is a little less than 15%. You can see why they didn't offer maturities for longer than 6 years.

THE DISCOUNTED RATE OF RETURN WITH MULTIPLE FUTURE SUMS

Finding the discounted rate of return when only one future sum is involved isn't too difficult, but let's see what happens when more than one future sum is involved.

Problem 5-10:

The purchasing agent for the accounting firm of Dewey, Cheatum and Howe was contemplating the purchase of a new 12-digit electronic calculator with built-in alarm clock and automatic pencil sharpener. The old machine it replaced would be donated to charity. The agent estimated that the new machine would save his firm $120 in the first year, $130 in the second year, $140 in the third year, and $150 in the fourth year, because of repair costs on existing equipment that would not have to be made if they purchased the new calculator. If the calculator costs $400, lasts four years, and will have no salvage value or disposal cost, what will be the rate of return on this investment?

Solution:

There are no short cuts this time. Now we simply have to guess at a discount rate and try it. Bear in mind that we still want to find a rate that will equate the present value of the future savings with today's $400 outlay. We'll try 10% for a starter:

Year	Savings	pvf at 10%	Present Value of Savings
1	$120	.9091	$109.09
2	130	.8264	107.43
3	140	.7513	105.18
4	150	.6830	102.45
		Total present value	$424.15

$424.15 is too large. To make this smaller, we need to use a larger discount rate. Any interest rate will do, so let's just go to 12% and see if we get any closer.

Year	Savings	pvf at 12%	Present Value of Savings
1	$120	.8929	$107.15
2	130	.7972	103.64
3	140	.7118	99.65
4	150	.6355	95.33
		Total present value	$405.77

That was fairly close so we'll try 13.0% and see what happens.

Year	Savings	pvf at 13%	Present Value of Savings
1	$120	.8850	$106.20
2	130	.7831	101.80
3	140	.6931	97.03
4	150	.6133	92.00
		Total present value	$397.03

Now that we have the answer bracketed between 12% and 13%, let's split the bracket and try 12.5%.

Year	Savings	pvf at 12.5%	Present Value of Savings
1	$120	.8889	$106.67
2	130	.7901	102.71
3	140	.7023	98.32
4	150	.6243	93.65
		Total present value	$401.35

Since the initial outlay of $400 is between $401.35 and $397.03, a simple interpolation yields 12.66% as our rate of return. (Try this interpolation on your own to see if you've finally got the technique.) Since it is always a good idea to check your work, we'll do it now by setting up a present value table for 12.66% and discounting the future savings.

Year	Savings	pvf at 12.66%	Present Value of Savings
1	$120	.8876	$106.51
2	130	.7879	102.43
3	140	.6993	97.90
4	150	.6208	93.12

Total present value $399.96

Since $399.96 is reasonably close to the initial $400 outlay, we conclude that our interpolation gave us a fairly accurate rate of return.

Did you realize that we simplified the problem by assuming that all of the *outlays* were incurred in year zero? A more common case is one in which the expenditures are also stretched out into the future; then it is necessary to find the discount rate that will equate the present value of the cash revenues with the present value of the cash expenditures.

Problem 5-11:

Suppose that the purchasing agent in Problem 5-10 was allowed to spread the $400 equipment cost over a four-year period. He would pay $100 right now and $100 in each of the next three years. What is the discounted rate of return under these conditions?

Solution:

A discount rate must be found that will equate the present value of the returns with the present value of the outlay. This time, however, the present value of the *costs* are also dispersed over time. Since the answer to Problem 5-10 was 12.66%, we might as well start with this.

Year	Expenditures	Savings	pvf at 12.66%	Present Value of Expenditures	Present Value of Savings
0	$100	0	1.0000	$100.00	0
1	100	$120	.8876	88.76	$106.51
2	100	130	.7879	78.79	102.43
3	100	140	.6993	69.63	97.90
4	0	150	.6208	0	93.12
				$337.18	$399.96

Obviously 12.66% does not equate the present value of the expenditures with the savings. We must try a much higher discount rate. After *much* trial and error it appears as if 31.5% is close to our rate of return on investment, as the computations below illustrate:

Year	Expenditures	Savings	pvf at 31.5%	Present Value of Expenditures	Present Value of Savings
0	$100	0	1.0000	$100.00	0
1	100	$120	.7605	76.05	$ 91.26
2	100	130	.5783	57.83	75.18
3	100	140	.4398	43.98	61.57
4	0	150	.3344	0	50.16
				$277.86	$278.17

By the way, we could have worked the problem by taking the difference between the revenues and the costs in each period and then discounting the difference. We didn't because we wanted to emphasize that future costs, as well as revenues, must be discounted.

The consequence of spreading the payments out into the future was to increase the rate of return on the investment. The total payments were the same, but the better yield resulted from the *timing* of the payments. Instead of having to part with $400 immediately, only $100 was paid in year zero, and the remainder could be invested in other alternatives until such time as the next payment was required. Stretching the costs out into the future results in a lower present value of those costs, hence the higher rate of return in the problem. If we treat all costs as negative cash flows, we can illustrate Problem 5-11 in Figure 5-1.

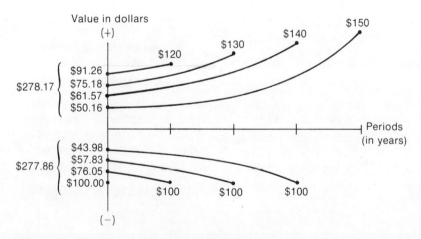

Figure 5-1. Problem 5-11: Equating the present value of the savings with the present value of the costs, using a 31.5% discount rate.

Figure 5-1 also typifies the way in which many cost-benefit problems are analyzed. In the case of a particular investment project, the first task would be to identify the future "benefits" (anticipated revenues) and then the costs, so that both can be discounted back to the present. The rate of return on the project can be found by finding the rate that will equate the present value of the benefits with the present value of the costs. Or, a single discount rate can be used to discount the revenues and the costs so that a ratio of costs to benefits (hence the term cost-benefit analysis) can be determined.

SUMMARY

In this chapter we have examined the third of our four major time value concepts, that of the discounted rate of return. In essence, we have tried to find the discount rate that could be used to make the present value of a given future payment equal to a given payment today.

In the case of a single future sum, two methods of solution were used. The first involved an algebraic solution based on the time value of money equation and takes the form of the discount rate of return equation (5-1) below:

$$r = \sqrt[n]{\frac{S_n}{S_0}} - 1.$$

This is a relatively simple expression and can be easily solved if our calculator has an exponential power key.

Our second method of solution was based on the observation that any present value factor represents the ratio of present to future sum as expressed in (5-2) below:

$$pvf = \frac{S_0}{S_n}.$$

As long as we can find the present value factor, and as long as we know the discount period, n, we can use the table to search along the appropriate period row until we find the value for r. This method usually involves interpolation but for the most part this alternative method of finding the discounted rate of return can be very useful.

In the case of multiple future sums, we had to resort to our third method of solution, that of trial and error. This method is more time consuming, but as long as we are not working with an annuity, it's as good a way as any to find the solution.

ADDITIONAL PROBLEMS

1. Suppose that you have $275 today and you make a deposit in an account that compounds the interest annually. If you close the account and withdraw $556.12 in exactly 16 years, what interest rate was paid to you during that period?

    Answer: 4½%

2. If an old friend was only able to pay back $32 of the $50 you loaned him five years ago, what was the annual rate of return on this investment?

    Answer: -8.54%

3. If you have an account that compounds interest monthly and has an effective annual yield of 5.64%, what is the stated annual interest on the account?

    Answer: 5½%

4. What would be your rate of return if you held your $100 Honus Wagner card (Problem 5-2) for 60 years and sold it for $20,000? (If your calculator has an exponential key you're in luck.)

    Answer: 9.23%

5. A 3-year Lone Stare certificate of deposit with the Texas State Bank in West, Texas compounds interest quarterly and requires a $1000 deposit. If you receive $1268.23 at maturity, what is the real, or effective, annual rate of return?

    Answer: 8.24%

6. What if *you* had bought the Honus Wagner card last year for $100 and you had an offer to sell it for $3000 today? What would be your rate of return on investment?

    Answer: 2900%

7. According to *Long Term Economic Growth*, a publication of the U.S. Department of Commerce, the implicit price deflator for GNP was 31.7 in 1874 and 108.8 by 1964. If your favorite money and banking professor wanted to know the annual compounded rate of inflation for this period, what would you tell him?

Answer: 1.38% per year

8. If the purchase of a new $4500 knucklebolt will save $5000 by the end of this year, $3000 at the end of the next, and $1000 at the end of each of the next three years when it will be worn out and worthless, what is the rate of return on this investment?

Answer: 66.75%

CHAPTER 6

THE DISCOUNT PERIOD

In this chapter we are going to examine the fourth and last time value concept discussed in Table 1-1, that of the discount period. Now we want to find the amount of time, whether it be minutes, months, or millennia, that separates the present and the future sums. This time span is called the discount period and, like the other time value concepts discussed earlier, is named after the unknown variable in the time value equation.

The structure of this chapter is similar to previous ones. We'll begin with the general case of a single future sum and examine two ways in which the discount period can be found. In the latter part of the chapter, we will deal with problems that have more than one future sum.

THE DISCOUNT PERIOD WITH A SINGLE FUTURE SUM

Using the Algebraic Solution. The algebraic solution used in this chapter is basically the same as the one used earlier; we simply try to isolate the unknown term by setting the known variables equal to it and then solve the equation.

First, we begin with our time value expression

$$S_n = S_0 (1 + r)^n,$$

and then divide both sides by S_0, which gives us

$$(1 + r)^n = \frac{S_n}{S_0}. \qquad (6\text{-}1)$$

Now we have a problem: it is difficult to arrange the equation in a way to isolate the unknown term, n, by itself. Instead, we'll leave the equation as written in expression (6-1) and call it our *discount period equation.*

Let's try a problem, one with some familiar values, to see how we use the discount period equation to solve for n.

Problem 6-1:

Be the first kid on your block to own a new $236.74, 20 BHP @ 5000 RPM, 40cc, OHC, chromo-flash moped, with rally stripe and reclining seat optional! Trouble is, you only have $100 in a 9% savings account which is compounded annually. How long will it be before you can buy it?

Solution:

We'll need our calculator for this problem, but first we'll write the discount period equation and fill in some of the values:

$$(1 + .09)^n = \frac{S_n}{S_0}$$

$$= \frac{\$236.74}{\$100} = 2.3674.$$

Next we'll go to our calculator and multiply 1.09 by itself until we reach 2.3674. Again, our steps:

Arithmetic	Algebraic

Arithmetic

1. set for floating decimal

2. constant key on

3. enter 1.09

4. press $\boxed{\text{x}}$ key

5. press $\boxed{\pm}$ key until 2.3674 appears in the display.

Algebraic

1. enter 1.09

2. press $\boxed{\text{x}}$ key

3. press $\boxed{=}$ key until 2.3674 appears in the display.

or:

1. enter 1.09

2. press $\boxed{x^y}$ key

3. enter some random value for n

4. press $\boxed{=}$ key

5. if the answer is larger than 2.3674, repeat steps 1 through 4 and use a smaller n; if the answer is too small, use a larger n.

If your calculator has a constant feature, the value of 2.3674 appears in the display when the $\boxed{=}$ key is depressed for the ninth time. If your calculator has an exponential power key, and does *not* have the constant feature, you simply have to search for the appropriate value for n. In either case, the value for n in this problem is 10; we therefore conclude that the discount period is equal to *ten* years.

You probably realize that the solution above is not an algebraic one in the true sense of the word, but it is an approximation that will serve us well and is as close to an algebraic solution as we will get with this type of problem.

Of course, we can't always count on finding the exact value for the term $(1 + r)^n$ in our calculator display, as the next problem illustrates. When this happens, we have to estimate the answer by interpolating.

Problem 6-2:

At one point during the attempts to reorganize seven financially troubled railroads in the northeastern United States, a value of $587,300,000 was placed on the assets of these railroads by the U.S. Railway Association, a federal agency managing the government-mandated reorganization. The figure was derived by assuming a $3.6 billion scrap value of the assets, less $1.8 billion in various liquidation expenses such as continued administrative costs, tearing up the roadbed, dismantling material, preparation for sale as scrap, and so on. This left $1.8 billion to be received after liquidation. The $587,300,000 is the *present value* of this $1.8 billion future payment. If the Railway Association used an 8% discount rate, how long did they expect the liquidation to last?

Solution:

Well, if $587,300,000 is the present value of $1,800,000,000 sometime in the future, then we can use our discount period equation:

$$(1 + .08)^n = \frac{S_n}{S_0}$$

$$= \frac{\$1.8000}{\$.5873} = 3.0649.$$

Now we go the the calculator and multiply 1.08 by itself until we reach 3.0649. Our steps:

Arithmetic	Algebraic
1. set for floating decimal	1. enter 1.08
2. constant key on	2. press $\boxed{\times}$ key
3. enter 1.08	3. press $\boxed{=}$ until 3.0649 appears in the display.
4. press $\boxed{\times}$ key	
5. press $\boxed{\begin{smallmatrix}+\\=\end{smallmatrix}}$ key until 3.0649 appears in the display.	

This time we didn't find 3.0649 in the display. Instead we found 2.9372 in the 14th period and 3.1722 in the 15th period. Since the answer is between these two limits, we'll simply interpolate.

$$
1 \text{ period} \left\{ x \left\{ \begin{array}{l} \text{14th period, } (1.08)^{14} = 2.9372 \\ \text{nth period, } (1.08)^n = 3.0649 \end{array} \right\} .1277 \right\} .2350 \\ \text{15th period, } (1.08)^{15} = 3.1722
$$

$$
\frac{x}{1 \text{ period}} = \frac{.1277}{.2350},
$$

$$
x = .5434 \,(1 \text{ period}) = .5434 \text{ periods.}
$$

Finally,

$$
\text{nth period} = 14 \text{ periods} + x
$$

$$
= 14 \text{ periods} + .5434 \text{ periods} = 14.54 \text{ periods.}
$$

The liquidation would last about 14½ years.

Is an answer of "about 14½ years" accurate enough? The answer is that the accuracy usually depends on the problem. In this case it's still an open question whether or not the $587,300,000 constitutes even a reasonable approximation of the value of the railroads. This method, for instance, valued Penn Central at $471.2 million while the trustees of Penn Central claimed a value of $7.4 billion, over 15 times the value assigned by the U.S. Railway Association. The courts should settle it sometime this decade, or perhaps the next.

We're going to work one more problem before we try to solve for the discount period by using the table in the Appendix. While you are working the problem, bear in mind that our method for finding n in expression (6-1) works for *all* discount rates, even those you can't find in the table.

Problem 6-3:

Against the rather insistent objections of your wife, five years ago you decided to invest a modest $1500 in a little Amalgamated International Industries common stock. Ever since then, the value of your investment has decreased 8% per year. Although you feel that you'll be all right in the long run, you did compromise and promise your wife that you would sell out if the investment ever fell to one-half the original value. If it keeps losing value at 8% per year, how many years do you have left before you are forced to keep your promise to your wife?

Solution:

We'll begin by writing expression (6-1) and then we'll fill in the values.

$$(1 + r)^n = \frac{S_n}{S_0}$$

$$(1 - .08)^n = \frac{\$750}{\$1500}$$

$$(.92)^n = \frac{\$750}{\$1500} = .5000$$

By repeatedly multiplying .92 times itself, we find a value of .5132 in the 8th period and a value of .4722 in the 9th period. If you made your investment 5 years ago you've got less than 4 years left. If you care to interpolate, you'll find you have about 3 1/3 years left before you are forced to sell.

This concludes our discussion of the algebraic method. Bear in mind that the approximation method works for any discount rate, positive or negative, and that the value for n (unless it is exceptionally large) can be found quickly if your calculator has a constant feature.

Using the Present Value Table. Our second method of finding the discount period involves the use of the present value table to look up the value for n.

In each of the discount period problems worked in this chapter, we knew the value for the present sum, S_0 and the future sum, S_n. We also know from expression (5-2) that the ratio of present to future value is the present value factor,

$$pvf = \frac{S_0}{S_n}.$$

If the discount rate is also known, we simply use the information given in the problem to find the present value factor and then we go to the table to look for the factor under the appropriate discount rate.

Problem 6-4:

Can you use the present value table to search for the discount period in the moped problem (Problem 6-1) at the beginning of the chapter?

Solution:

Of course! Recall that you had $100 in a 9% savings account and that you needed $236.74 to make your purchase. You already have values for three of the variables: S_0 = $100, S_n = $236.74, and r = 9%. First, we find our present value factor:

$$pvf = \frac{S_0}{S_n}$$

$$= \frac{\$100}{\$236.74} = .4224.$$

Then, we look *down* the 9% column until we find .4224 in the 10th period row. We have our answer: you would have to leave your money in the savings account for 10 years before the $100 grew to $236.74.

That wasn't hard, was it? Just use the available information to find the present value factor and then look it up in the table. Of course, they won't all be quite that easy; many of the present value factors we need won't be in the table so we'll have to interpolate to find our answer.

Problem 6-5:

Find the discount period in Problem 6-2 (the railroad problem) using the table. Recall that S_0 = $.5873 billion, S_n = $1.8 billion, and r = 8%.

Solution:

Using the present value factor expression (5-2), we write:

$$pvf = \frac{S_0}{S_n}$$

$$= \frac{\$587,300,000}{\$1,800,000,000} = .3263.$$

We've already been told that the discount rate is 8% so we go to our table and look *down* the 8% column until we find the present value factor of .3263. The answer is between the 14th period (pvf = .3405) and the 15th period (pvf = .3152), so we interpolate to find the answer:

$$
1\ \text{period}
\begin{cases}
x
\begin{cases}
14\text{th period, pvf} = .3405 \\
n\text{th period, pvf} = .3263
\end{cases}.0142 \\
15\text{th period, pvf} = .3152
\end{cases}.0253
$$

$$\frac{x}{1 \text{ period}} = \frac{.0142}{.0253}$$

$$x = .5616 (1 \text{ period}) = .5616 \text{ periods.}$$

Finally,

$$\text{nth period} = 14 \text{ periods} + x,$$

$$= 14 \text{ periods} + .5616 \text{ periods} = 14.56 \text{ periods.}$$

Aside from a minor difference of .02 periods, this is the same answer we got earlier.

In the next problem, we'll set up the solution so that it can be solved either way, by using the algebraic approach or by using the present value tables to search for n.

Problem 6-6:

Let's return to the time traveler we left jailed in Problem 2-8. If the authorities hadn't been sharp enough to notice the error in the date, how many trips would he have had to make to raise the $50,000 he needed? Remember that he started out with $4750 and planned to keep his money in several 4% savings accounts that compounded the interest annually.

Solution:

In other words, we need to know how long it will take the $4750 to grow to $50,000 at 4%. If we use equation (6-1), we get

$$(1 + .04)^n = \frac{S_n}{S_0}$$

$$= \frac{\$50,000}{\$4750} = 10.5263.$$

You could use your calculator to find the power to which 1.04 must be raised in order to equal or approximate 10.5263. Or, you could find its reciprocal, the present value factor:

$$\text{pvf} = \frac{S_0}{S_n}$$

$$= \frac{\$4750}{\$50,000} = .0950.$$

Now that we have the factor, we look in the table under 4% and we find it in period—oops! We don't find it. But you know what to do, don't you?

Remember, multiplying any two present value factors gives the factor for the sum of the two periods. If our factor is .0950, what two factors in the 4% column do we need to multiply to give us this value? To find the answer, simply take any factor in the 4% column and divide it into .0950; the result will be the factor for the period remaining.

If we can begin with any factor, let's use the factor for 50 periods (.1407) to find the factor for the remaining period.

$$\frac{.0950}{.1407} = .6752$$

If we look for the .6752 factor in the 4% column, we will find it between the 10th and 11th period rows. Interpolation reveals that the value for n is 10.02 periods. This means that the total discount period for the problem is 50 plus 10.02 periods, or 60.02 periods. Therefore, a 60-year deposit requires *six* 10-year trips in the time machine.

Now you know how to use the table to find a discount period that isn't listed. Of course, if the remaining present value factor still can't be found in the table after the initial division by the fifty year factor, simply divide it again—chances are that the discount period is more than 100 periods long. This method will work as long as the discount rate that you need to use is listed in the table.

THE DISCOUNT PERIOD WITH MULTIPLE FUTURE SUMS

Each of the preceding problems in this chapter had one thing in common: a *single* future sum,, S_n. These problems are usually quite easy to solve and they don't really get difficult until more than one future sum is involved. When we have multiple future sums, it's simpler to resort to the trial and error method.

Problem 6-7:

Family tradition dictates that your oldest daughter will be the first to marry. The next to eldest daughter will marry the year after that and the youngest three years after that. If you plan to spend $5000 on each wedding, and if you are presently funding these future plans with $10,000 CD that pays 7½% interest compounded annually, how soon will it be before the *first* wedding can be held?

Solution:

The three weddings will cost $15,000 in the future, but these payments occur in different years. We can't use the formula since there are three future sums involved, but we can use a technique we tried earlier, that of trial and error.

It's only a guess, but let's assume that the first wedding will take place in 5 years, the second in 6, and the last in 9. We need to discount each $5000 expenditure to the present and see if the sum of the expenditures can be funded by the purchase of a $10,000, 7½% CD today.

Year	Future Cost of Wedding	pvf at 7½%	Present Cost of Wedding
5	$5000	.6966	$3483.00
6	5000	.6480	3240.00
9	5000	.5216	2608.00
			$9331.00

Five years is close, but you won't need to wait that long. Let's see what happens if we move the first wedding up to 4 years.

Year	Future Cost of Wedding	pvf at 7½%	Present Cost of Wedding
4	$5000	.7488	$3744.00
5	5000	.6966	3483.00
8	5000	.5607	2803.50
			$10,030.50

That's even closer, but it's too soon. If we interpolate using 4 and 5 years as our limits, we'll find that the first wedding can be held in about 4 years and 16 days.

It turned out that our two guesses were pretty close, but this won't always be the case. As you can see, the problem could get even more difficult if we added more future sums, or even spread the future sums farther apart. Trial and error will usually work, given enough trials, but fortunately there is yet another method for dealing with multiple future sums as we shall see below:

Problem 6-8:

You have recently become interested in a *very* attractive divorcee and are contemplating marriage. To demonstrate your good intentions, she is asking you to invest in an 8%, $5000 CD that will be used to pay a $9000 tuition bill due when her young son enters college at age 19. The remainder of the money in the account will be used to buy him a $7000 car when he graduates 4 years later. How old is her son?

Solution:

Assuming that you are not intimidated by this rather unusual proposition, there are several ways in which it could be solved. You could try the trial and error technique, but let's try something different this time. We'll discount $7000 for four years at 8%, then *add* it to $9000 and treat them both as a single lump sum. Once we make this conversion (and it might help to look ahead at Figure 6-1 while we solve the problem), we can use the present value table to find the discount period.

First we discount $7000 for four periods at 8% (and we'll let the subscripts stand for the age of the son):

$$S_{19} = S_{23}(pvf)$$

$$= \$7000(.7350) = \$5145.$$

When her son is 19, you'll need $9000 to meet the anticipated tuition costs in addition to the $5145 needed to buy the car 4 years later, a total of $14,145. If this is the future sum you will need n periods in the future, we can now find the present value factor:

$$pvf = \frac{S_0}{S_n}$$

$$= \frac{\$5000}{\$14,145} = .3535.$$

Looking *down* the 8% column, we find .3535 between the 13th and 14th periods. Interpolating, we find that the discount period is roughly 13½ periods, so her son must be 5½ years old.

If we look at Figure 6-1 below, we can get a clearer picture of the way in which we solved problem 6-8 above. Since both future expenditures ($9000 at age 19 and $7000 at age 23) can be funded by a $14,145 lump sum at age 19, all we had to do was find the number separating the $5000 today from the lump sum in the future. Of course we didn't know what our lump sum was until we first found the value of the $7000 expenditure four years earlier ($5145), and then added it to $9000.

When we get to the chapter on annuities, we'll use this technique of condensing future expenditures to a future lump sum rather extensively.

SUMMARY

This discussion of the discount period concludes our examination of the four time value concepts discussed in Table 1-1. As we have seen, we are trying to find the amount of time that separates present and future sums that have equivalent present values.

In the case of a single future sum, we discovered that two methods of solution are possible. The first, our algebraic solution, is based on the time value equation and takes the form of the discount period equation (6-1) below:

$$(1 + r)^n = \frac{S_n}{S_0}.$$

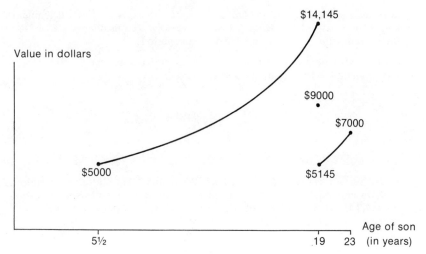

Figure 6-1. Problem 6-8: Condensing multiple future expenditures into a single future sum.

However, we did not try to isolate the exponent, n, by itself. Instead we tried to approximate it with another method; we simply multiplied the term $(1 + r)$ times itself until we got close enough to the value of $\dfrac{S_n}{S_0}$ to interpolate.

The second method of finding the discount period is based on expression (5-2), which tells us that any present value factor represents the ratio of the present to the future sum:

$$pvf = \frac{S_0}{S_n}.$$

As long as we know the discount rate and can find the present value factor, we can go to the tables and search down the appropriate discount rate column until we find the discount period or are able to interpolate for it.

In the case of multiple future sums, we found that the trial and error method could be of use, as well as a new method by which we condensed the future payments into a single future sum. As we shall see, this new method will be extremely useful to us in the next chapter.

ADDITIONAL PROBLEMS

1. If your great-granddaddy opened a $500 savings account on your behalf when you were born, and if you just found out that the account had a value of $1621.70, how old are you if the deposit has been compounding at a 4% annual rate?

Answer: 30 years

2. Contrary to your high expectations, you reluctantly concluded that the rare stamp collection you paid $400 for some time ago is going to continue to depreciate in value at an annual rate of 9% per year. If another collector just offered you $188.10, how long have you owned the collection?

Answer: 8 years

3. The last time we looked, our colony of *Bacillus megaterium* was still growing like a weed. If the colony had 18,114 cells before lunch and is still growing at the rate of 2% a minute, how long a lunch break did we take if we found a colony of 107,652 when we got back? (Hint: the tables don't have enough periods.)

Answer: 90 minutes

4. In Problem 6-7, we had three future wedding expenditures of $5000 each. If each of these future expenditures were condensed into a single future sum at the time of the first wedding, how large would this sum be?

Answer: $13,395.

5. In many primitive societies, non-productive livestock serves as a symbol of wealth, but the consumption of goods to support this livestock without a corresponding economic benefit makes them, in fact, a considerable burden instead of actual wealth. To help alleviate this problem, a Central Camel Bank, complete with interest-bearing deposits and a fractional reserve system to lessen the total number of camels, has been proposed for the nomadic herdsmen of Arabia. (With a fractional reserve system of 20%, a deposit of one million camels could be backed by an actual reserve of only 200,000 camels, while only 150,000 camels would be needed if the reserve requirement was lowered to 15%.) As long as the Central Camel Bank was in charge of the reserve rate, camel procreation would take on an entirely new meaning—a change in the reserve rate could create more camels than a ton of Conceptuol. Instead of discussing problems of fertility, health, and mortality with your herdsman, you would discuss interest rates, security, and life insurance for camels with your banker.

If you have a herd of only 300 camels and your neighbor, who owns 500 camels, is always bragging about having a larger herd, how long would you have to leave your camels in the bank at 12% in order to have the same number of camels as your neighbor, whose herd size is stable?

Answer: slightly more than 4½ years

CHAPTER 7

ANNUITIES: PART I

An annuity is a fixed sum paid or received at uniform intervals over a period of time. Insurance premiums, pension benefits, mortgage payments, car payments, some preferred stock dividends, and even an occasional lottery prize are just a few examples of annuity payments.

The concept of an annuity is very simple, but the range of problems is so broad that it is necessary to deal with the topic in two chapters instead of one. In this chapter we'll deal primarily with the present and future values of an annuity. Later in the chapter we'll examine some annuity formulas and in a brief appendix we'll look at the yield to maturity on a bond and compare this to its true rate of return. In the next chapter, we'll deal with other topics such as the amount of annuity (size of each periodic payment), duration of annuity (the number of periods the annuity will last), and the discounted rate of return.

The major difference between these two chapters and previous ones is that now we will be working with multiple future sums of equal size instead of single future sums or multiple sums of different amounts. The time value concepts, however, are the same as those in the first six chapters, as we will discover below.

THE PRESENT VALUE OF AN ANNUITY

We already found the present value of one annuity in Problem 3-10, when we discounted three separate $1100 payments at 6% to find their total present value. If you will recall, we set up the problem like this:

$$S_0 = \frac{\$1100}{(1 + .06)^1} + \frac{\$1100}{(1 + .06)^2} + \frac{\$1100}{(1 + .06)^3} .$$

Mathematically, it makes no difference whether we divide $1100 three times by the appropriate number and then add the terms, or first factor out the $1100 common term and write the problem like this instead:

$$S_0 = \$1100 \left(\frac{1}{(1 + .06)^1} + \frac{1}{(1 + .06)^2} + \frac{1}{(1 + .06)^3} \right) .$$

87

With the common term factored out of the expression, we are left with three present value factors within the parentheses. We could further simplify the problem by reducing each present value factor to its decimal equivalent and then adding them together:

$$S_0 = \$1100 \; (.9434 + .8900 + .8396)$$

$$= \$1100 \; (2.6730).$$

Now look in the back of the book behind the present value table at the table called "Present Value of Annuity Factors," (p. 149) and find the factor for 3 periods at 6%. You will find 2.6730, the number you derived above when you added the present value factors! Each *present value of annuity factor* or *pvaf* in this table was found that way. This point is important:

The present value of annuity factor (pvaf) for any period n is the sum of the present value factors for periods 1 through n.

Any time we have the annuity factor, the solution to the problem is greatly simplified. For example, if we are trying to discount a stream of equal future payments back to the present, we simply multiply the annual payment by the annuity factor found in the table:

$$S_0 = \text{annuity (pvaf)}. \qquad (7\text{-}1)$$

Now we can use expression (7-1), which we call the *present value of annuity equation*, to finish the annuity problem we discussed above. With an annuity of $1100 and a factor of 2.6730 for 6%, 3 periods, we have

$$S_0 \doteq \text{annuity (pvaf)}$$

$$= \$1100(2.6730) \;\; = \$2940.30.$$

Aside from a $.03 error due to rounding, this is the same answer obtained earlier in Chapter 3, and the computation is less tedious.

Every now and then you won't have an annity table to work with so you should be aware of a way to compute any present value of annuity factor with your calculator.

Problem 7-1:

Using your calculator, find the annuity factor for 9% in the fifth period.

Solution:

If your calculator has a memory the answer is easily computed. Since the equation for the present value factor for any period n at 9% is

$$\frac{1}{(1+.09)^n} \ ,$$

simply compute the following steps*:

Arithmetic	Algebraic

Arithmetic

1. set for floating decimal
2. constant key on
3. enter the numerator "1"
4. press ⌹ key
5. enter 1.09 (for 1 + 9%)
6. press ⌹ key
7. press M+ key
8. repeat steps 6 and 7 four more times and recall the answer from memory (which should be 3.8897).

Algebraic

1. enter numerator "1"
2. press ⌹ key
3. enter 1.09 (for 1 + 9%)
4. press = key
5. press M+ key
6. repeat steps 4 and 5 four more time and recall the answer from memory (which should be 3.8897).

If your calculator has an automatic summation key instead of the M+ key, the computation is even easier because each present value factor is automatically added into the memory as it appears in the display.

Looks pretty simple, doesn't it? To find the present value of annuity factor for any ordinary annuity, we sum the present value factors and we have our answer. We could even do the same for various discount rates and time periods and arrange the factors in a convenient table such as that found in the back of this book. Of course, as long as you know how to use your calculator, you can find any present value of annuity factor, even if it isn't listed in the table.

We do have a table at the end of this book, but we must remember that it is based on the assumption that the first annuity payment is made at the *end* of the first time period, something known as an *ordinary annuity*. Frequently, however, payments on insurance policies, magazine subscriptions, and other annual payments are made in advance at the *beginning* of the time period. This is called an *annuity due*, which is nothing more than an ordinary annuity plus an initial payment. Perhaps the best way to see the difference between the ordinary annuity and the annuity due is by examining Figure 7-1.

---

*The formula for the present value of an ordinary annuity factor appears in the brackets in expression (7-5) on page 106 of this chapter. The formula is convenient if the problem involves a large number of periods, but you won't be able to solve it quickly unless your calculator has an exponential power key. If you don't have the exponential key, use the steps in the problem.

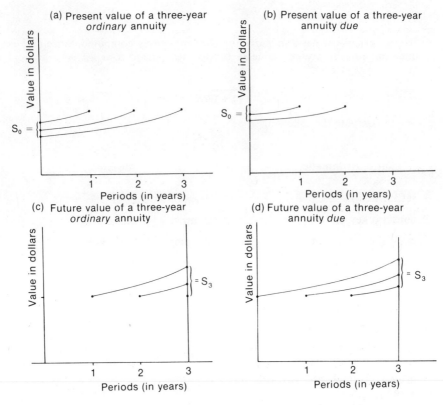

Figure 7-1.   Ordinary and annuities due, present and future values.

For example, in part (a) of Figure 7-1 we see a 3-year ordinary annuity in which the first payment takes place at the end of the first year. In order to find the present value of this annuity, S_0, each of the three payments must be discounted to the present and then added. In the case of the 3-year annuity due in part (b), there are only two future payments to be discounted before they can be added to the initial payment (already a present value), so that the total present value can be found. In other words, the 3-year annuity due is the same thing as a 2-year ordinary annuity, plus initial payment.

Having alerted you to this difference, we want to mention that from now on all annuities, unless otherwise specified, are assumed to be *ordinary annuities*. Even the table at the end of this text is for ordinary annuities, although the word "ordinary" does not appear in the title.* Now we can try a few problems to get the feel of it.

---

*If you happen to need an annuity due factor, turn to the ordinary annuity table in the appendix, subtract one period from the number of payments in the annuity and add 1 to the factor you find in the table. If you need a factor for 10 periods at 7½%, turn to the table and find the factor for 9 periods (which is 6.3789) and add 1 to it. The annuity due factor for 10 periods, 7½%, is 6.3789 + 1, or 7.3789.

Problem 7-2:

The ticket you bought last week in the new state lottery really paid off: $10,000 per year for the next 20 years!

If you ignore Uncle Sam and other freeloading relatives, what is the present value of this annuity if your best alternative is to put all of your money in an 8% savings account?

Solution:

The annuity is $10,000, the duration is 20 years, and the discount rate is 8%. If you look in the annuity table under 8%, 20 periods, and find the annuity factor of 9.8181, you can set up the problem using expression (7-1):

$$S_0 = \text{annuity (pvaf)}$$

$$= \$10,000(9.8181) = \$98,181.$$

The current value of your $10,000, 20-year annuity discounted at 8% is $98,181.

Don't forget that all of the problems such as the one above involve *ordinary* annuities unless otherwise specified. The next problem is a little longer but is basically the same. If nothing else, it provides a little insight into an interesting problem.

Problem 7-3:

When faced with a state prohibition against the open burning of leaves, residents of a town in southern New York elected to collect their leaves into large piles for composting and use the resulting compost on municipal grounds or sell it commercially. The town is a residential area with a higher than normal share of trees that generates some 40,000 cubic yards of semicompacted leaves annually. This amounts to 6,000 tons of leaves, which would otherwise cost $129,000 to dispose of in a nearby Connecticut landfill, the cheapest alternative to composting.

The collection and composting program required eight vacuum machines, one shredder, and ten specially constructed boxes for an initial cost of $63,000. This equipment was expected to last eight years and have an annual maintenance cost of $4000. An additional $15,000 in labor and other cash expenses had to be spent each year, but the sale of compost generated $5000 annually. If the town figures that capital costs the municipality 6½%, will the present value of the returns exceed the present value of the costs?

Solution:

The returns are the net annual savings effected by not having to haul the leaves to Connecticut. With additional annual labor costs of $15,000 and additional maintenance costs of $4000 balanced by annual savings of $129,000 for not hauling leaves, $110,000 could be saved. If we add in the $5000 revenue from compost sales, the compost decision will be $115,000 cheaper than the hauling solution for each of the eight years; in effect, an eight-year annuity. We find the present value by using the annuity factor for 8 periods, 6½%, and discount as follows:

$$S_0 = \text{annuity (pvaf)}$$

$$= \$115,000(6.0888) = \$700,212$$

The present value of the annual savings will be *far* greater than the $63,000 present value of the costs.

Always try to remember that the annuity factor represents the *sum* of the present value factors. If any payments are missing, you'll have to adjust the annuity factor by subtracting the present value factors for those periods in which no payments are received. Here's a situation you might be faced with at one time or another:

Problem 7-4:

Assume that you are twenty years old, a senior in college, and are considering an M.B.A. program that takes one year to complete. You have also been told that someone who holds an M.B.A. earns about $3000 per year more than someone who holds a B.S. Using a discount rate of 8½%, what is the present value of the extra income your would receive over the course of your lifetime if you decided to get the M.B.A. and retire at age 65?

Solution:

The extra $3000 received by the holder of M.B.A. is only a rough estimate, but we can consider this as an annuity for the purposes of this problem.

The problem is that the annuity doesn't start right away since you'll be in school one more year and you'll miss the annuity payment for the first year.

Well, if an annuity factor is the sum of the present value factors, we use the annuity factor for 45 periods at 8½% and subtract the present value factor for the period in which no extra income is received (in this case the first year. If you missed payments in other years, you would have to subtract the present value factors for these years as well). If we use subscripts to designate the specific periods for the factors, the problem would appear as

$$S_0 = \text{annuity} (\text{pvaf}_{45} - \text{pvf}_1)$$

$$= \$3000(11.4653 - .9217)$$

$$= \$3000(10.5436) = \$31,630.80.$$

$31,630.80 is the present value of the additional lifetime income we attributed to the M.B.A. degree.

Of course the present value of the additional income, the $31,630.80 above, is only part of the picture. If you decided to go to graduate school you would have to incur additional expenses such as books, tuition, and lost income. The next step (which we will not pursue at this point) would be to find the present value of these costs and compare them to the present value of the benefits.

Another common type of annuity problem is one that deals with the market price of a bond.

Problem 7-5:

Five years ago the Waldenburg Wonder Widget Corporation sold a number of 6¼%, 25-year bonds that pay interest semiannually. Since then, interest rates went up and the yield to maturity on these triple A-rated bonds rose to 9%. What is the current market price of a $1000 par value Widget bond today?

Solution:

The current price of the bond has two parts, the present value of the future semiannual interest payments, and the present value of the $1000 principal that will be paid in 20 years. (It was a 25-year bond 5 years ago, now it's a 20-year bond.)

Interest paid semiannually will amount to one-half of $1000 times 6¼%, or $31.25 every six months for 40 periods. The formula used by the investment industry discounts these semiannual payments at *one-half* of the yield to maturity, or 4½%:*

$$S_0 = \text{annuity (pvaf)}$$

$$= \$31.25(18.4016) = \$575.05.$$

The 40-period annuity ($31.25 paid twice each year) has a present value of $575.05. To find the present value of the $1000 paid at maturity in 20 years, we discount this amount by the present value factor for 4½%, 40 periods:

$$S_0 = S_n \text{ (pvf)}$$

$$= \$1000(.1719) \quad = \$171.90.$$

The market price for this triple-A bond maturing in 20 years is $575.05 plus $171.90, or $746.95.

---

*A yield of 4½% semiannually is not the same as an annual yield of 9%. The yield to maturity found with the tables and calculators used in the investment industry for bond computations will not give you a true annual rate of return. Because of this, bond yields *cannot* be directly compared to rates of return on other investments, a topic which is discussed in more detail in the appendix to this chapter.

An interesting use of annuities is seen in the case of lifetime subscription to magazines or memberships in professional organizations. We obviously have an annuity problem here; the difference is that there is a cost involved rather than a revenue.

Problem 7-6:

At the time of this writing, a popular national magazine subscription was $8.50 per year or $200 for a lifetime membership if the subscriber is age 10 or older. Would it be cheaper for you, a white male age 20, to subscribe on an annual basis or pay the lifetime subscription rate? If you didn't buy the lifetime subscription, you could invest your $200 elsewhere and get a 7½% return. (Now we've got an *annuity due*; the first payment is due at the start of the first time period, before any of the issues are received.) A life expectancy table tells us that the average 20-year old white male has 50.1 years left.

Solution:

Since the first payment must be made right away, its present value is $8.50. That leaves 49 more payments, a 49-year *ordinary* annuity. If we find the present value of these remaining payments, we can add the two present values to get our answer. Turning to the table, we find the factor of 12.9479 under the 7½% column, 49th period row. To find our present value, we write

$$S_0 = \text{annuity (pvaf)}$$

$$= \$8.50(12.9479) = \$110.06.$$

The present cost of a lifetime subscription that is paid in 50 annual payments of $8.50 amounts to $8.50 plus $110.06, or $118.56, considerably less than the $200 lifetime rate offered by the magazine. Or, had you decided to follow the suggestion in the footnote on page 90, you could have gone to the ordinary annuity table to find the factor of 12.9479. You then add 1.0000 to get the annuity due factor of 13.9479. When this factor is multiplied by $8.50, the answer of $118.56 is found.

Of course, if you decide to keep the $200, you might not be able to get a 7½% return on your money. Suppose that the best available alternative is a 5% savings account, how would this alter your conclusion? Well, if you look in the annuity table under 5%, 49 years, you'd find a factor of 18.1687. If we repeat the steps in the above problem, we'll find its present value to be $162.93. Since this is still less than the $200 present cost of the lifetime subscription, it would be better to buy it yearly.

Why do some people buy lifetime subscriptions? Obviously we've overlooked the very important factor of inflation; we made the unlikely assumption that in 50 years the annual subscription rate will still be $8.50. A lifetime subscription is one hedge against future price increases. Even so, is there anyone in your family who might live long enough to take advantage of the lifetime rate?

Problem 7-7:

We already know that you would be better off to renew your subscription as it comes up each year, but what about your kid sister who just turned 10? Would she be better off to withdraw $200 from her 5% savings account and pay the lifetime rate, or would she be better off to renew on a yearly basis? (A quick check with the life expectancy tables reveals that your sister has 67 years left.)

Solution:

We have a 67-period annuity due that can be converted to a 66-period ordinary annuity plus an initial payment. The problem is, our tables only go as far as 50 periods, so what do we do now? We can't multiply annuity factors as we did earlier with our present value factors, nor can we add or divide to find an annuity factor greater than 50 periods.

Simple! we'll separate the 66-year annuity into a 50-year annuity (that we can solve with our table) and a 16-year annuity that begins 50 years from now. If we use the annuity factor for 16 years at 5%, we can find the lump sum value of the last 16 payments in the 50th year, which we will call S_{50}. (It might help to look ahead to Figure 7-2 for this step.)

$$S_{50} = \text{annuity (pvaf)}$$

$$= \$8.50(10.8378) = \$92.12$$

Now we have the value of a 16-year annuity starting in 50 years, but what is its value today? With the help of our present value tables, we can discount this sum, which exists 50 years hence, back to its present value:

$$S_0 = S_{50}(\text{pvf})$$

$$= \$92.12(.0872) = \$8.03.$$

So, $8.03 is the present value of a 16-year, $8.50 annuity that begins in 50 years. It only remains to find the present value of the 50-year ordinary annuity:

$$S_0 = \text{annuity (pvaf)}$$

$$= \$8.50(18.2559) = \$155.18.$$

We've broken the problem into three parts, so all we have to do is add the present values and we'll have our answer. First, we have the $8.50 initial payment, next we have the $8.03 present value for the last 16 years and finally we have the $155.18 present value of the first 50-year part of the annuity: a total present cost of $171.71 for the 67-year annuity. This is still not large enough to warrant the lifetime rate of $200.

If you'll examine Figure 7-2, you can see the way in which we handled one of the parts to the problem. Since our annuity table wasn't long enough to handle the last 16 years, we had to collapse this part of the annuity into a single lump sum, and then discount this sum back to the present.

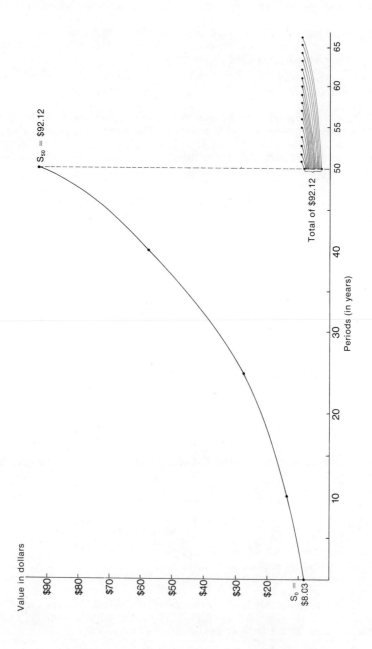

Figure 7-2. Problem 7-7: Condensing a future annuity to a single future sum.

Once we found the present value of the 16-year annuity 50 years from today to be $8.03, we added it to the present value of the 50-year annuity and the $8.50 initial payment to give us our total present value. If the duration or length of the annuity was 100, or even 150 years, you could handle the problem the same way; condense the future annuity to a future lump sum and discount that sum to its present value.

Of course, even this method won't work in the case of forever, or *perpetual* annuities, so we'll have to try something else. Fortunately, the answer is in our table,,so all we need to do is look. Run your eye down any column in the annuity table and you'll notice that the change in the pvaf from one period to the next is longer in early periods and smaller in later ones. This should be expected since payments in early periods are worth more than payments in later ones. As we look down any column around the 40 to 50 period row, we see that the annuity factor changes very little from one period to the next; in fact, it appears as if each of the annuity factors is reaching some limit. The annuity factor will approach that limit as the number of periods approaches infinity.

But what is the limit? If we go over to the 20% column, we find that the annuity factor approaches 5 as a limit. In the 25% column, the annuity factor approaches 4 as a limit. The factor that is the limit in each case is simply the reciprocal of the discount rate! Or, we could express the perpetual annuity factor as

$$\text{limit}_{n \to \infty} \text{pvaf} = \frac{1}{r}, \tag{7-2}$$

which means that the annuity factor approaches $\frac{1}{r}$ as a limit when n approaches infinity. When the annuity lasts forever, the annuity factor for 20% is 5 and the annuity factor for 25% is 4, just as 100 is the annuity factor for a perpetual annuity discounted at 1%.

Let's use the perpetual annuity factor in (7-2) to finish the subscription problem above:

Problem 7-8:

If you lived forever, what would be the present value of an $8.50 perpetual annuity discounted at 5%?

Solution:

Since the annuity factor for a *perpetual* annuity is the reciprocal of the discount rate, we write

$$S_0 = \text{annuity} \left(\frac{1}{r}\right)$$

$$= \$8.50 \left(\frac{1}{.05}\right)$$

$$= \$8.50(20) = \$170.$$

How about that! Even if you lived forever, the present value of the $8.50 ordinary annuity wouldn't reach $200! (Of course, this is a magazine subscription, and hence an annuity *due*, so we'll have to add the initial $8.50 cost of today's payment. If you lived forever, the present value of the perpetual annuity *due*, would be $170 plus $8.50, or $178.50.)

Naturally you won't live forever, but you should realize that occasionally you will find a problem in which the discount rate and the number of periods are sufficiently large so that the problem can be treated as if it were a perpetual annuity even though it isn't. There will be some error involved, but this may be permissible, depending on the problem you are attempting to solve.*

---

*The amount of error can be expressed as a percentage of the actual present value by setting up the problem as follows (note that we have to use the present value of annuity factor bracketed in expression (7-5) on page 106):

$$\text{error as a \% of actual present value} = \frac{\text{perpetual annuity factor} - \text{annuity factor}}{\text{annuity factor}}$$

$$= \frac{\frac{1}{r} - \left[\frac{1 - \frac{1}{(1+r)^n}}{r}\right]}{\frac{1 - \frac{1}{(1+r)^n}}{r}} = \frac{1 - \left[1 - \frac{1}{(1+r)^n}\right]}{1 - \frac{1}{(1+r)^n}} = \frac{\frac{1}{(1+r)^n}}{1 - \frac{1}{(1+r)^n}} \qquad (7\text{-}3)$$

$$= \frac{1}{(1+r)^n - 1} \qquad (7\text{-}3a)$$

The percentage error, then, is equal to $\frac{pvf}{1 - pvf}$ as we have in (7-3). If you don't have tables with the appropriate factors, (7-3) can be further simplified to yield (7-3a) which you will find easier to solve with your calculator.

For example, suppose that you treated the 66-year, 5% ordinary annuity in Problem 7-7 as a perpetual annuity. We already know that the actual value is $8.03 plus $155.18, or $163.21, and we know that the value if treated as a perpetual annuity is $170. The difference between the two valuations is $6.79 or, when expressed as a percentage of the actual present value, $6.79/$163.21 = 4.16%. If we had used expression (7-3) instead, we would have (where the pvf for 66 periods is the product of the pvf for 50 and 16 periods):

$$\frac{pvf}{1 - pvf} = \frac{.0399}{1 - .0399} = \frac{.0399}{.9601} = .0416 = 4.16\%.$$

Or, if we wanted to use (7-3a), we would have

$$\frac{1}{(1+r)^n - 1} = \frac{1}{(1 + .05)^{66} - 1} = \frac{1}{25.03 - 1} = .0416 = 4.16\%.$$

The answer is the same.

Our next problem involves an insurance policy with two annuities (in fact, most insurance problems also involve annuities *due* because of the timing of the first payment).

Problem 7-9:

Your brother-in-law, who sells insurance as a sideline, is trying to get you interested in a nifty little retirement policy. Starting today, you will have to pay $600 annually until retirement at age 65; the day you retire, you will begin to receive $5000 annually until death. If retirement is 22 years away and you plan to live long enough to collect 10 annual payments, would you be interested? (Your alternative is to invest in 6% CDs, so use this as your discount rate.)

Solution:

We'll approach the problem by finding the present value of the annual cost, and then we'll compare it to the present value of the benefits.

As for the costs, you will shell out $600 right away and $600 at the end of each year for 21 additional years. Using a 6% discount rate, the value of the ordinary 21-year annuity is

$$S_0 = \text{annuity (pvaf)}$$

$$= \$600(11.7641) \quad = \$7058.46.$$

If we add in the initial $600, the policy will have a present cost of $7658.46. (It might help to look ahead at Figure 7-3 while we work the problem.

What about the present value of the expected benefits? If you do live ten years after retirement, then you will have a ten-year, $5000 annuity sometime in the future.

Since the first payment is 22 years away, we have a 10-year annuity *due* starting 22 years from now. However, *ordinary* annuity table assumes that the first payment is made one year (or period) in the future. Since you will still receive 10 annual payments of $5000, the ordinary annuity table will give you the lump sum value of this annuity one year *before* the first payment, 21 years from now. If the ordinary annuity starting in 21 years is the same as an annuity due starting in 22 years, we can use the ordinary annuity factor for 6%, 10 periods, to find the value of these 10 annual payments 21 years from today:

$$S_{21} = \text{annuity (pvaf)}$$

$$= \$5000(7.3601) \quad = \$36,800.50.$$

If it is worth $36,800.50 in 21 years, what is it worth today? We'll use the present value table and the 6%, 21-period factor to find out..

$$S_0 = S_{21} \text{ (pvf)}$$

$$= \$36,800.50(.2942) \quad = \$10,826.71$$

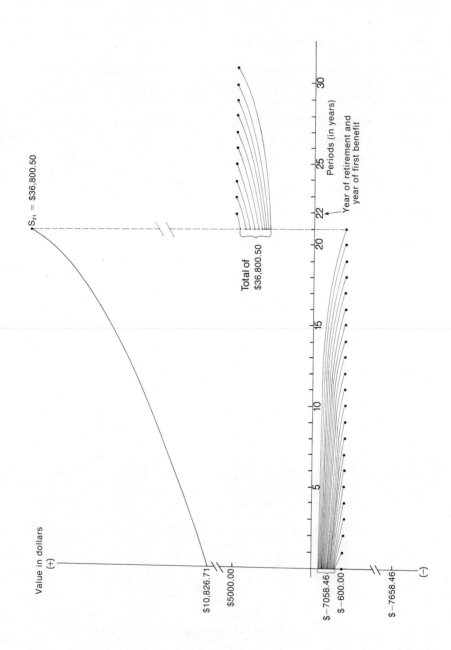

Figure 7-3. Problem 7-9: Comparing the present values of a future annuity benefit and a future annuity cost.

With a present value cost of $7658.46 and present value benefits of $10,826.71, the policy seems to be worthwhile.

Before we abandon this problem, look again at Figure 7-3 to make sure you understand the way in which we turned the ten-year annuity *due* into an *ordinary* annuity. Remember that the table for ordinary annuities assumes that the first payment is made at the *end* of the first year. The ten-year annuity due in Problem 7-9 started in the 22nd year, but this is the same as a ten-year *ordinary* annuity starting in the 21st year, which allows us to use the ordinary annuity table to solve this part of the problem.

So much for insurance, let's try something else, like a bond problem. This time we're going to see if we can reduce the government debt.

Problem 7-10:

By early 1976, the U.S. Treasury had exhausted its legal authority to issue more than $10 billion worth of long-term bonds paying over 4¼% interest. Since 4¼% interest was well below the market rate, and since the $10 billion authority had long been used up, no new long-term bonds were being issued and the Treasury found itself being forced into shorter term debt. In February of 1976, the Treasury Secretary asked Congress to permit the issue of an *additional* $10 billion in long-term debt, with yields in excess of the 4¼% ceiling.

If the Treasury was given the authority to issue an additional $10 billion of 7%, 20-year bonds, and if the proceeds of this issue were used to retire part of an old issue of 4% bonds paying interest annually and maturing in 1996 yielding 7% to maturity, how much new *short-term* debt could the Treasury issue without increasing the national debt? (Short-term debt is not affected by the $10 billion ceiling, only the long-term debt.)

Solution:

That's obvious! Since $10 billion would be *issued* and $10 billion would be *retired*, the Treasury could issue no more short-term notes without increasing the national debt, right?

Wrong! Look again at how much debt would be retired.

If the old debt pays 4% annually, yields 7%, and matures in 20 years, then the present value of the $40 interest annuity for each $1000 of principal is

$$S_0 = \$40 \, (pvaf)$$

$$= \$40(10.5940) = \$423.76.$$

And each $1000 of principal discounted to present value at 7% would be worth

$$S_0 = \$1000 \, (pvf)$$

$$= \$1000(.2584) = \$258.40.$$

We find that each $1000 of old bond issue is going for $423.76 plus $258.40, or $682.16. How much is going for $10 billion? Since each dollar obtained from the sale of the new bonds can be used to retire $1000/$682.16, or $1.466 of old bonds, then the entire $10 billion obtained from the sale of the new bonds can be used to retire $14.66 billion of old debt and the national debt would go *down* by $4.66 billion with a sleight-of-hand paper shuffle.

Now that the national debt has been reduced by $4.66 billion, the Treasury could issue an *additional* $4.66 billion in new, short-term notes and put the nationl debt back where it started with no apparent increase or decrease, but with almost $5 billion more in the Treasury.

After the issue of $4.66 billion in new short-term debt, could the national debt possibly be the same? Well, yes and no. The national debt as it is usually measured gives only the principal amount of federal debt and this figure would not increase. But this represents only one dimension of the value of our national debt. We must also consider the future commitment to pay interest, the different timing of future payments (both principal and interest), and changing interest rates. We must, in other words, consider the *present value* of the national debt, which is not the same thing as the principal value of that debt. So while this refunding scheme would not increase the national debt as it is now measured, it would increase its present value by $4.66 billion.

THE FUTURE VALUE OF AN ANNUITY

All of the annuity problems discussed so far have been concerned with finding the *present* value of a future income stream. Occasionally, however, we want to know the *future* value of an annuity or the value to which the annuity payments will accumulate at the end of the annuity.

We'll begin our discussion by referring back to Figure 7-1 to examine the two diagrams in the bottom part of our figure. As we can see, we still have two basic types of annuities: the ordinary annuity in part (c) and the annuity due in (d). Each annuity has a duration of 3 periods and again, the only difference is in the timing of the first payment. In both cases, however, we are looking for the future value of all annuity payments in some year n.

We'll start with a problem and illustrate the technique for finding future value.

Problem 7-11:

The Teacher's Insurance and Annuity Association is a tax-deferred retirement fund used by many college and university faculty. Teachers contribute to the fund during their working years and accumulate credits to their individual accounts. At retirement the accumulated amount can be used to buy a life annuity, an annual payment for as long as the participant lives. (This arrangement is much like the insurance policy described in Problem 7-9).

If the fund manages to maintain a 7½% return in the future, and if a 35-year old teacher contributes $500 at the end of each academic year, how much will be in his fund account when he retires at the end of the academic year at age 65?

Solution:

You could solve the problem by compounding the first $500 for 29 years at 7½%, the second $500 for 28 years, the next for 27 years, and so on for each of the 30 deposits, but there's an easier way (and it might help to look ahead at Figure 7-4 while we work the problem).

Instead, let's treat the $500 payments as an ordinary annuity and find the present value of the 30 payments discounted at 7½%:

$$S_0 \quad = \quad \text{annuity (pvaf)}$$

$$= \ \$500(11.8104) \quad = \ \$5905.20.$$

The $5905.20 is the value of the annuity today, but what will it be worth in 30 years, the day of the last payment? Now we use our *present* value factor for 30 years at 7½% to find the *future* value of this sum:

$$S_{30} \ = \ \frac{S_0}{\text{pvf}}$$

$$= \ \frac{\$5905.20}{.1142} \quad = \ \$51{,}709.28.$$

You should have a small fortune of $51,709.28 in your fund account when you retire.

See how we find the future value of an annuity? We simply collapse the annuity back to a lump sum in the present and then find its future value. Figure 7-4 illustrates this for the problem above. As you can see, the problem only involves two steps: first we find the present value of the annuity, then we find its future value. Even if the problem involves an annuity due, the solution is the same.

Let's try a problem involving an annuity due just to make sure we can solve it.

Problem 7-12:

You've been giving it a lot of thought and you've decided that in four years you're going to trade your wife in for a younger model (right now she's putting you through school).

If, starting today, you deposit $10 a month in a 6% account for the next 4 years, will you have enough to finance a $500 divorce when you graduate? (Interest is compounded monthly.)

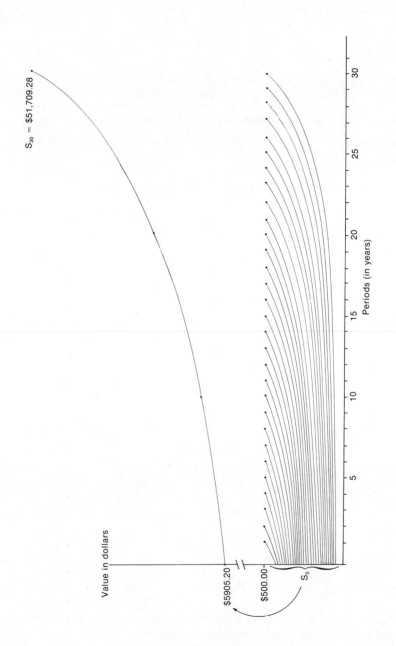

Figure 7-4.   Problem 7-11: Finding the future value of an ordinary annuity.

Solution:

Forty-eight monthly deposits, starting today, is the same as a 47-period annuity plus the initial payment. Since the interest per period is 6%/12, we look in the .5% column, 47th period row to find our annuity factor of 41.7932, which we use to find the present value of the annuity:

$$S_0 \ = \ \text{annuity (pvaf)}$$

$$= \ \$10(41.7932) = \$417.93.$$

If we add in the initial $10 payment, the 48-period annuity due has a present worth of $427.93. This value compounded ahead for 48 periods at .5% has a future value of

$$S_{48} \ = \ \frac{S_0}{\text{pvf}}$$

$$= \ \frac{\$427.93}{.7871} \ = \ \$543.68.$$

Assuming that you don't change your mind, you should even have $43.68 left for a farewell party.

As you can see, the only difference between finding the present and future values of an annuity is the extra step of compounding the present lump sum into the future, which we can summarize with the *future value of annuity equation* below:

$$S_n \ = \ \frac{\text{annuity(pvaf)}}{\text{pvf}} = \text{annuity}\left(\frac{\text{pvaf}}{\text{pvf}}\right) \qquad (7\text{-}4)$$

Like the compound interest tables, we don't need future value of annuity tables. The present value of annuity factor divided by the present value factor *is* the future value of annuity factor. In fact, this method is really so simple that we don't need to work any more problems in this section. Instead we'll move on to a brief discussion of annuity formulas.

ANNUITY FORMULAS

Throughout the course of this book, we have emphasized the need to understand the problem and we have minimized the short cut solutions that use equations to grind out the answers. Many texts, for example, include both future as well as present value tables when only one is needed.

When we come to the topic of annuities, there is a tendency to have a proliferation of formulas. If you have another textbook handy, one that discusses annuities and other time value concepts, chances are that it will have a formula for the present value of an ordinary annuity that looks like this:

$$S_0 = \text{annuity} \left[\frac{1 - \dfrac{1}{(1+r)^n}}{r} \right] . \tag{7-5}$$

The formula itself can be derived by thinking of an ordinary annuity as consisting of a perpetual annuity starting now, less a perpetual annuity starting in year n. The perpetual annuity starting now will have a value of

$$\text{annuity} \left(\frac{1}{r} \right),$$

while the present value of the perpetual annuity beginning in year n would be the value of the perpetual annuity discounted to the present by the present value factor in year n.

$$\text{annuity} \left(\frac{1}{r} \right) \left[\frac{1}{(1+r)^n} \right]$$

Therefore, the present value of the annuity running only to year n would be equal to the difference between the two:

$$S_0 = \text{annuity} \left(\frac{1}{r} \right) - \text{annuity} \left(\frac{1}{r} \right) \left[\frac{1}{(1+r)^n} \right]$$

$$= \text{annuity} \left(\frac{1}{r} \right) \left[1 - \frac{1}{(1+r)^n} \right] = \text{annuity} \left[\frac{1 - \dfrac{1}{(1+r)^n}}{r} \right] .$$

Again we have expression (7-5), which is the formula for the present value of an ordinary annuity.

The expression within the brackets in (7-5) above is the formula for a present value of an ordinary annuity factor. If you care to take out your calculator and experiment, you'll find that any of the factors in the annuity tables can be computed with this formula. Then again, we could also compute any factor in the table by first finding, and then adding, the values for the individual present value factors. If you will recall, this is where we began our discussion of annuities, with the observation that any present value of annuity factor, or *pvaf* for short, is equal to the sum of the present value factors.

When we came to the section on future value of annuities, we observed that any annuity could first be condensed to a present sum and then compounded into the future with the use of the present value factor. We summarized this operation with the future value of annuity equation (7-4) below:

$$S_n = \text{annuity}\left(\frac{\text{pvaf}}{\text{pvf}}\right)$$

Since the equation for a present value factor is $\dfrac{1}{(1+r)^n}$, let's divide this into expression (7-5) and see if we can derive the equation for the future value of an ordinary annuity

$$S_n = \text{annuity}\left(\frac{\text{pvaf}}{\text{pvf}}\right) = \text{annuity}\ \frac{\left[\dfrac{1-\dfrac{1}{(1+r)^n}}{r}\right]}{\dfrac{1}{(1+r)^n}} = \text{annuity}\left[\dfrac{1-\dfrac{1}{(1+r)^n}}{r}\right](1+r)^n$$

$$= \text{annuity}\left[\dfrac{(1+r)^n - \dfrac{(1+r)^n}{(1+r)^n}}{r}\right] = \text{annuity}\left[\dfrac{(1+r)^n - 1}{r}\right] \tag{7-6}$$

Our last term above, expression (7-6), is the standard formula for finding the future value of an ordinary annuity.

We could even show you two more formulas, one for the present value of an annuity due and one for the future value of an annuity due. This would give us one formula for each of the four types of annuities illustrated in Figure 7-1.

We could, but we won't. Instead we'd rather have you keep something simpler in mind. As long as you realize that an annuity is just a stream of equal payments occurring at uniform intervals, you'll have no problem. Pay attention to the timing of the first payment so that you don't get confused between an annuity due and an ordinary annuity. Above all, remember this: if you are looking for the present value of an annuity, you only need one set of tables for both kinds, ordinary or due, since one can be converted into the other. If you need the future value of an annuity, condense it into a present lump sum and compound it into the future. The answer is the same and it's a lot easier.

SUMMARY

In this chapter, we have examined ways to find the present and future lump sum values of an annuity. Annuities, as we have seen, are periodic payments of equal size made for a specified length of time.

When finding the present value of the annuity, we simply multiply the annuity by the present value of annuity factor,

$$S_0 = \text{annuity(pvaf)},$$

where the present value of annuity factor is the sum of the present value factors in periods 1 through n.

Because of the timing of the first payment, annuities are sometimes categorized two ways: the *ordinary* annuity has its first payment made at the *end* of the first period, and the annuity *due* has its first payment made at the *beginning* of the first period. However, the timing of the first payment does not pose any difficulty; as we have seen, we can simply convert the annuity due into an ordinary annuity plus an initial payment and use our table in the appendix to solve either problem.

Occasionally you may want to find the future value of an annuity. When this is the case, we first find the present value of the annuity, and then compound it ahead to the appropriate year with the use of the present value factor. In short:

$$S_n = \text{annuity} \left(\frac{\text{pvaf}}{\text{pvf}} \right).$$

Finally, we paused to comment on the proliferation of formulas that can occur whenever annuities are discussed. We did derive the formulas for the present as well as the future value of an annuity, but it is not uncommon to find four formulas, one for each of the annuities found in Figure 7-1. In fact, many books even include a series of tables in the appendices for each type of annuity. However, as long as you pay attention to the timing of the first payment, and as long as you know how to convert the present value of an annuity into a future one, one table is all you'll ever need.

ADDITIONAL PROBLEMS

1. Find the present value of a 20-year, $2000 ordinary annuity discounted at 10%.

    Answer: $17,027.20

2. What is the present value of a 20-year, $2000 annuity *due* if the 10% stated annual interest is compounded annually?

    Answer: $2000 times 9.3649, or $18,729.80.

3. What is the present value of annuity factor for 7¼%, 10 periods?

    Answer: 6.9431

4. Calculate the present value of a $300, 12-period annuity discounted at 8¼% per period.

    Answer: $2231.83

5. Hambone, your good-looking dog, recently won a beauty contest and was awarded a 10-year supply of dogfood, $31.75 worth, delivered at the end of each month. If you would like to sell this prize and put the proceeds in a 10-year, 12% finance company note that compounds interest monthly, how much would you ask for the dog food? (Hint: set your calculator for floating decimal and use expression 7-5.)

    Answer: $2212.99

6. On your first birthday, Aunt Agnes started putting $10 in your 5% savings account and continued this practice until your 21st birthday. She had some hard times, however, and missed payments on your 8th and 13th birthdays. If you haven't made any withdrawals, how much will you have in your account tomorrow when you celebrate your 24th birthday?

    Answer: $374.52

7. If your kid sister valued her money at 7% instead of 5% in Problem 7-7, how large an error would you have if you treated the 66-year part of the annuity as a perpetual annuity? (Hint: use expression 7-3 or 7-3a.)

    Answer: 1.16% of the actual present value

8. You have a savings account that pays 10% stated annual interest, compounded semiannually. If you plan to withdraw $2000 at the end of each year for the next 20 years, how much do you have in the account today? (Hint: this is *not* a 20 period, 10% annuity.)

    Answer: $16,740.57

APPENDIX

YIELD TO MATURITY, SEMIANNUAL COMPOUNDING, AND THE TRUE RATE OF RETURN ON A BOND.

We wanted to deal with the topic of bond yields in a separate section because we have found that a bond's yield to maturity is commonly confused with its true annual rate of return. Since most bonds pay interest semiannually, the future interest and principal payments are discounted to the present using one-half the yield to maturity. Because, for example, a 4% yield for 10 periods is not the same as an 8% yield for 5 periods, the yield to maturity understates the bond's true yield much the same way that the stated annual interest on a passbook savings account understates the true yield if the interest is compounded daily, monthly, or quarterly.

In actual practice, bond brokers, bankers, investment managers, and others who deal with bonds on a regular basis don't discount each future payment to find the current price of a bond. Instead they use bond calculators or bond tables similar to the one in Figure 7-5. For example, if we wanted to find the current price of the Waldenburg Wonder Widget bond in Problem 7-5, we could turn to the sample bond page found in our illustration, look down the twenty year column until it intersects the 9% row, and find the value of 74.70. The price of our 20-year Widget bond yielding 9% to maturity is $747.00 according to our bond value table. If our bond table had enough pages, columns, and rows (for coupon rates, years to maturity, and yields), we could look up the price of virtually and bond that pays interest semiannually.

These tables, as well as the pre-programmed calculators used in the investment community compute the present value of the bond using the assumption that the semiannual rate is one-half the yield to maturity. In general, the expression (where the yield to maturity is defined as y_m and n stands for the number of half-year periods) is:

110

$$\begin{matrix} \text{current} \\ \text{price} \end{matrix} = \begin{matrix} \text{semiannual} \\ \text{interest} \end{matrix} \left[\frac{1}{(1 + \frac{y_m)}{2}} + \frac{1}{(1 + \frac{y_m)^2}{2}} + \cdots + \frac{1}{(1 + \frac{y_m)^n}{2}} \right]$$

$$+ \text{ principal} \left[\frac{1}{(1 + \frac{y_m)^n}{2}} \right] \qquad (7\text{-}7)$$

This is the equation used to find the price of the bond in the Widget problem and it is also the equation used to generate each of the bond prices in Figure 7-5.

Yield to Maturity	Years to Maturity			Coupon Rate: 6¼%
	19½	20	20½	21
8.00	82.86	82.68	82.51	82.34
8.10	82.02	81.83	81.65	81.47
8.20	81.18	80.99	80.80	80.62
8.30	80.36	80.16	79.96	79.78
8.40	79.55	79.34	79.14	78.95
8.50	78.75	78.54	78.33	78.14
8.60	77.96	77.75	77.54	77.34
8.70	77.19	76.97	76.75	76.55
8.80	76.43	76.20	75.98	75.77
8.90	75.68	75.44	75.22	75.01
9.00	74.93	74.70	74.47	74.26
9.10	74.20	73.96	73.73	73.51
9.20	73.48	73.24	73.01	72.78
9.30	72.78	72.53	72.29	72.07
9.40	72.08	71.83	71.59	71.36
9.50	71.39	71.14	70.89	70.66
9.60	70.71	70.45	70.21	69.97
9.70	70.04	69.78	69.54	69.30
9.80	69.38	69.12	68.87	68.63
9.90	68.73	68.47	68.22	67.98

Figure 7-5. Sample page from a bond value table.

When it comes to finding a true annual rate of return, however, we can't simply double the semiannual rate ($y_m/2$), even though this is the method used by the investment community to compute the yield to maturity. To find the true annual rate, the semiannual rate must be *compounded* for two periods. In the case of our bond problem, the y_m was defined as 9% and the semiannual rate ($y_m/2$) was 4½%. Compounding our semiannual rate for two periods yields 9.2%, not the 9% yield to maturity in the problem. (A 4½% semiannual rate will cause $100 to grow to $100 $(1.045)^2$ or $109.20 in one year. This is a true annual rate of 9.2%.)

If we are interested in defining the 9% yield in the Widget problem as a *true* annual yield (or y_t), then we could find the semiannual rate with the help of expression (5-1), our rate of return equation:

$$r = \sqrt[n]{\frac{S_n}{S_0}} - 1.$$

If S_0 is the value at the beginning of a one-year period and S_n the value at the end, then the S_n/S_0 term in (5-1) can be replaced with the expression $1 + y_t$, since one plus the true yield is the ratio of a value at the start of a year to the value at the end of the year. Thus our semiannual rate of return will be

$$r_{semiannual} = \sqrt[2]{1 + y_t} - 1. \tag{7-8}$$

Now that we have found an expression that defines the semiannual rate when the yield to maturity is interpreted as a true annual rate, we can substitute expression (7-8) for $y_m/2$ in expression (7-7) to yield:

$$\frac{current}{price} = \frac{semiannual}{interest} \left[\frac{1}{\left(\sqrt[2]{1+y_t}\right)^1} + \frac{1}{\left(\sqrt[2]{1+y_t}\right)^2} + \dots + \frac{1}{\left(\sqrt[2]{1+y_t}\right)^n} \right]$$

$$+ principal \left[\frac{1}{\left(\sqrt[2]{1+y_t}\right)^n} \right] \tag{7-9}$$

If we had wanted to price the Widget bond to yield a true or effective 9% annual rate of return, it would have a current price of $761.99 instead of the $747.00 we found using the bond table.

Certainly you would not be indifferent to the difference between an investment opportunity that has a true 9% rate of return and a bond that pays interest semiannually and has a yield of 9% to maturity. Because of the semiannual compounding, the bond with a 9% yield to maturity (and a 9.2% true yield) is the better alternative.

Thus we see that the yield to maturity understates the true annual yield so that bond yields cannot be validly compared to rates of return on other investments that *are* stated in true annual rates. Obviously a set of bond value tables similar to the page displayed in Figure 7-5 based on equation (7-9) rather than (7-7) would remedy this problem.

ADDITIONAL PROBLEMS

1. What is the current price of a 25-year, $1000 bond that pays 5% interest semiannually and yields 7% to maturity?

    Answer: $25(23.4556) = $586.39
    $1000(.1791) = $179.10
    $765.49

2. If our $1000, 25-year, 5% bond yields 7% to maturity in the above problem, what is the true annual yield?

    Answer: $(1 + \frac{7\%}{2})^2 = 1.0712$ or 7.12%

3. In one of our earlier bond problems (Problem 3-11 on page 33), we made the simplifying assumption that 6% interest on the $1000, 4-year bond that yielded 8% to maturity is paid annually. What would be the price of the same bond if the interest payments were made semiannually?

    Answer: $30(6.7327) = $201.98
    $1000(.7307) = $730.70
    $932.68

4. Which of the following has a higher true yield: a 6 1/4% savings account that compounds interest daily, or a bond with a 6 3/8% yield to maturity paying interest semiannually?

    Answer: The bond has a slightly higher true yield of $(1 + \frac{6\ 3/8\%}{2})^2 = 1.064766$, or 6.48%. The savings account had a true yield of $(1 + \frac{6\ 1/4\%}{360})^{360} = 1.064489$, or 6.44%.

CHAPTER 8:

ANNUITIES: PART II

In the previous chapter, we spent some time with methods that allowed us to compute the present as well as the future values of an annuity. In this chapter we're going to work with problems involving the size or amount of the annuity, the duration of the annuity, and the discounted rate of return.

In fact, we'll see that the methodology employed in this chapter is familiar. Given any three of the four variables in an annuity problem (n, r, S_0, and the amount of the periodic payment), the fourth can always be found. Let's start with the amount of annuity below and see what we mean.

THE AMOUNT OF ANNUITY

Given the amount or size of a periodic payment, we know how to find its present value. Quite often we find that we want to go in the other direction: given a present value we want to find the amount of the repeated annual payment it would fund. For example, we might start our retirement with a tidy sum saved during our lifetime and want to find out how much we could pay out each year for the remainder of our expected life. Finding the size of the annuity is only a matter of rearranging equation (7-1) below:

$$S_0 = \text{annuity (pvaf)},$$

so that it appears as

$$\text{annuity} = \frac{S_0}{\text{pvaf}}. \qquad (8\text{-}1)$$

This new expression (8-1) is what we will call our *amount of annuity equation*. Let's see if we can use it to solve a little problem.

Problem 8-1:

In June, 1976 the South Carolina Watermelon Growers' Association awarded a talented bystander $50 for spitting a watermelon seed 25 feet and 7 inches, a feat which won first prize in a contest they sponsored. If our bystander puts the prize in a special 5% Fourth of July Watermelon Fund to purchase watermelons for an Independence Day party each year for the next 16 years, how much can he spend on watermelons each year and have nothing left after the 16th party? (The interest in the fund is compounded annually.)

Solution:

First of all, let's phrase the question like this: what size 5%, 16-year ordinary annuity has a present value of $50? We are given 5% and 16 years, so we look in the annuity table and find the annuity factor of 10.8378. Well, if any 16-year annuity discounted at 5% has a present value 10.8378 times the annual payment, then the annual payment must also be the present value ($50) divided by 10.8378:

$$\text{annuity} = \frac{S_0}{\text{pvaf}}$$

$$= \frac{\$50}{10.8378} = \$4.61.$$

Although 25 feet and 7 inches is a little short of a world record (which is a little over 40 feet), it's long enough to finance a $4.61 victory party each of the following 16 years.

The next problem is basically the same except for the timing of the first payment. As we shall see, expression (8-1) works equally well whenever we have a problem involving an annuity due.

Problem 8-2:

You have received a $200 debating award from the Consolidated Daughters of the American Bicentennial for the purpose of buying a lifetime subscription to the magazine of your choice (which just happens to cost $8.50 annually, with the first payment due today). If you instead decide to put the money in a 5% savings account and withdraw it in 50 equal annual payments, how much will you have left over each year after you pay the cost of the subscription? Remember that you are not only withdrawing interest, but interest and principal, so that you will have nothing left after 50 years.

Solution:

In other words, how much can you take out of a $200, 5% account each year for 50 years and have nothing left if the first withdrawal is made today? The solution can be determined as we did before, but first we need to convert our annuity due into an ordinary annuity by discounting the present $200 value of the annuity one period at 5%. (This will give us last year's value of a $200 present sum which we call S_1.)

$$S_{-1} = S_0 (pvf)$$

$$= \$200(.9524) = \$190.48$$

Since one period now separates the lump sum value of the annuity and the first payment, we have an ordinary annuity that began one year ago. Now we can use the amount of annuity equation and the annuity factor for 5%, 50 periods:

$$\text{annuity} = \frac{S_{-1}}{pvaf}$$

$$= \frac{\$190.48}{18.2559} = \$10.43.$$

Starting today, you will be able to make 50 equal withdrawals of $10.43 until nothing is left in your account. If you subtract the annual $8.50 subscription cost, you'll have $1.93 left over each year.

As long as you remember that any annuity due starting today is the same as an ordinary annuity starting one period ago, you should have no trouble with finding the size of the annual payment.

Here's another:

Problem 8-3:

United Bananas has agreed to sell its land in Panama to the Panamanian Government for $151,500. The land will be leased back to $2 million per year on a 5-year lease and is expected to produce 22 million boxes of bananas annually. If the value of the land is $20 million, and if United Bananas has an annual cost of capital of 10%, how much must the price of a box of bananas be raised if the loss on the sale of the land is to be recovered during the life of the lease?

Solution:

Well, since the land is worth $20 million and was sold for $151,500, the loss was $19,848,500.

$19,848,500 divided by five years gives us $3,969,700 to recover each year, right?

Wrong! The recovery will be made in five separate time periods in the future and *must be discounted*. The question should be rephrased: what size 5-year annuity (the increased banana price return at the end of each year) will have a present value of $19,848,500 (the loss on the sale of the land)?

The 10% cost of capital will be the discount rate, so we look in the annuity table under 10%, 5 periods to find the annuity factor 3.7908 which we use to find the annuity amount:

$$\text{annuity} = \frac{S_0}{\text{pvaf}}$$

$$= \frac{\$19,848,500}{3.7908} = \$5,235,966.02.$$

If we divide the annuity by 22 million boxes of bananas, this will give a price increase of 23.8¢ per box. (At 42 pounds of bananas per box, that is an increase of 57¢ per pound, if you care.)

Don't forget that most problems, despite their apparent complexity, can be solved if they can be separated into their component parts. For example, consider the following:

Problem 8-4:

In 1909 your uncle started a 4% savings account into which he deposited $100 each year until he jumped from a window high above Wall Street in 1929. It was believed at the time that he died penniless, but his will was recently found and it has been determined that you are sole beneficiary of his estate consisting of the aforementioned account. The will stipulates, however, that any beneficiary under age 25 (you are 18) will receive the benefits in four equal annual installments to fund a college education. If you started college in 1978 and expect to receive your first annuity payment the next year, how large was the annual payments? (Your uncle never made a deposit in 1929, so there were only 20 annual deposits made into the savings account.)

Solution:

This problem only *looks* complicated—it actually consists of three simple problems: finding the present value of the 20-year annuity, determining the future value of that present sum, and finding the amount of a 4-year annuity. (It may help to look at Figure 8-1 while you work through the solution.)

We'll start off by finding the 1908 value of the $100 annuity by using the annuity factor for 20 periods, 4%. (Remember that an annuity due in 1909 is the same thing as an ordinary annuity in 1908.)

$$S_{1908} = \text{annuity (pvaf)}$$

$$= \$100(13.5903) = \$1359.03$$

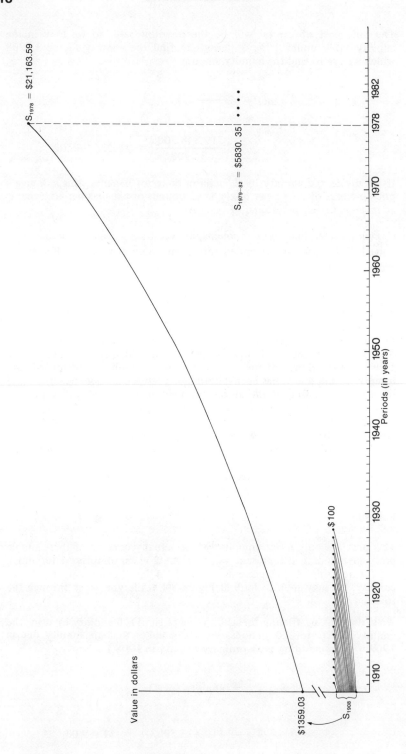

Figure 8-1.   Problem 8-4: Finding the amount of a four-year future annuity.

Now we have the 1908 value of the annuity, but what was it worth 70 years later in 1978? We already know how to use our present value factors to compound a sum into the future, so we'll just divide the 1908 sum by the present value factor for 50 periods and 20 periods (or any other combination of present value factors whose periods total 70) to find its value 70 years later:

$$S_{1978} = \frac{S_{1908}}{(pvf_{50})(pvf_{20})}$$

$$= \frac{\$1359.03}{(.1407)(.4564)} = \$21,163.59.$$

$21,163.59 is the accumulated value at the end of the compounding period, and it is the starting or present value for the second annuity as well. To find the size of this annuity, we use the annuity factor for 4 periods, 4%:

$$\text{annuity} = \frac{S_{1978}}{pvaf}$$

$$= \frac{\$21,163.59}{3.6299} = \$5830.35.$$

So $5830.35 is the size of the annuity left to you by your dear, departed uncle.

We've illustrated the solution to Problem 8-4 in Figure 8-1. Again, you can see the way in which the 20-year annuity due in 1909 was treated as a 20-year ordinary annuity in 1908.

Once we found the 1908 value of the annuity, it was a simple matter to compound it ahead for 70 years and then compute the size of the annuity payments.

Our next amount of annuity problem involves the common mortgage. Since a mortgage is repaid in equal periodic installments, it can be viewed as an annuity. Of course, if you borrow $10,000 from your local savings and loan association for 20 years at 6½%, it will be called a $10,000, 6½%, 20-year mortgage, not a $907.56, 20-year annuity (the size of the annual payment is computed with the 6½%, 20-period factor of 11.0185 in the tables). The $10,000 is the value of the mortgage the day it is signed, while the $907.56 annual payment is fixed by contract for 20 years. The holder of the mortgage has a promise to receive $907.56 each year for 20 years and the *present value* of this future income stream determines the value of the mortgage, *not* the fact that it was once worth $10,000.*

*The amount of the annuity is fixed and is not affected by the portion that goes to pay off the principal and the portion that goes to interest. However, if you should be interested in separating the $907.56 annual payment into interest and principal for any one year (for interest deduction on income tax, for instance), simply compute the principal

The value of a mortgage behaves much like the value of a bond, discussed in an earlier chapter. The current value of the mortgage, like the bond, will vary inversely with the interest rate. For example, if 5 years go by and mortgage rates stay at 6½%, the value of the $907.56, 15-year annuity will be $907.56(9.4027), or $8533.51. However, if mortgage rates go *up* to 8% by that time, the value of the $907.56, 15-year annuity will *fall* to $907.56(8.5595), or $7768.26, which is at a discount below its principal value.

If interest rates on comparable mortgages were to fall below 6½%, the mortgage would sell at a premium above its principal value. But then again, there might be times when some people would prefer that you didn't know about all of this, as the next problem illustrates:

Problem 8-5:

The First Federal Peoples Home Mortgage Security Savings and Loan Association issued an annual report in which total assets offset liabilities, as expected, at $15 million each. The assets included $13 million in first mortgage loans with an average yield of 7% and an average maturity of 12 years. At the time of the report, comparable mortgages were being written for 9½%.

The liabilities included $12 million in savings accounts. Are these accounts covered by the market value of the mortgage loans?

Solution:

What we really need to look at is the value of the $13 million mortgage part of the assets. Since the mortgage rate on the market is 9½%, we must discount the mortgages at 9½% to reflect the fact that a 7% mortgage is not worth its remaining principal in a 9½% market. If we are willing to accept the inaccuracies inherent in using averages instead of individual mortgages, we can find the present value of a $13 million, 7% mortgage paid in 12 annual installments by discounting at 9½%.

---

value at the beginning and at the end of the year. The difference is the amount of principal you paid off during the year and the rest of the annuity payment is interest. Of course, you are interested in the number of annuity payments remaining when you are computing the interest, not the number of payments already made.

For example, suppose that you are trying to find the amount of interest paid during the 16th year of a 20-year mortgage. Before you made the 16th payment, your mortgage had 5 payments remaining; with a value of $907.56(4.1557), or $3771.55. After the 16th payment was made, there were four remaining payments with a value of $907.56(3.4258), or $3109.12. The difference, $662.43, is the amount of principal paid off in the 16th year. If $662.43 of the $907.56 is payment on the principal, then $245.13 is the interest paid during the 16th year.

Another way to make the computation is with the present value table. Since the difference between a 5-period annuity factor and a 4-period annuity factor is the present value factor for the 5th period, we could use the present value factor for 5 periods at 6½% to find the amount of principal paid off in the 16th year. Or, .7299 times $907.56 is $662.43, the amount of principal paid off. The remaining $245.13 is the interest payment during the year.

Of course, we can't find the present value of this mortgage until we find the amount of the annuity, so we use expression (8-1) to find the annuity that would amortize a $13 million, 7% mortgage in 12 years:

$$\text{annuity} = \frac{S_0}{\text{pvaf}}$$

$$= \frac{\$13,000,000}{7.9427} = \$1,636,723.$$

A payment of $1,636,723 each year for 12 years has a present value of $13 million discounted at 7%. What present value does it have discounted at 9½%? We can find it easily enough if we use the annuity factor for 9½% at 12 years:

$$S_0 = \text{annuity (pvaf)}$$

$$= \$1,636,723(6.9838) = \$11,430,546.$$

This gives us a present worth of $11,430,546 for the mortgages instead of the $13,000,000 carried on the books. The present value of the mortgages, discounted at the current 9½% interest rate, is *not* enough to cover the $12,000,000 in savings accounts.

Remember, it is the annuity that is valued in a mortgage. Of course, any given annuity has a different present value for each discount rate and this is one way of inflating the value of your assets, as we have just seen.

Now let's take a look at the next topic in this chapter.

THE DURATION OF ANNUITY

In each of the problems in the previous section, the initial sum (S_0), the discount rate of return (r), and the discount period (n) were the factors used to find the size of the annuity. In this section we want to deal with problems in which the annuity amount is known, but not the annuity period.

By now the methodology should be readily apparent. All we need to do is to divide each side of expression (7-1) by the annuity to get our *annuity factor equation:*

$$\text{pvaf} = \frac{S_0}{\text{annuity}}. \qquad (8\text{-}2)$$

With the help of (8-2) and the annuity table, we can proceed to find the duration (the lifetime) of the annuity.

Problem 8-6:

A secret admirer left you a modest sum of $5000 which currently is on deposit in a 6½% account that compounds interest annually. If you decide to spend the money at the rate of $360 a year, how long will the money last?

Solution:

We'll use expression (8-2) and then fill in the values to get

$$\text{pvaf} = \frac{S_0}{\text{annuity}}$$

$$= \frac{\$5000}{\$360} = 13.8889.$$

Now we go to the annuity table and look *down* the 6½% column until we find a factor close to 13.8889. In the 37th period row we find a factor of 13.8879, so we conclude that the money will last a little more than 37 years.

Let's go back to the topic of mortgages, but this time we want to take a look at a mortgage with a variable interest rate.

Problem 8-7:

You have just been informed that your local Federal Savings and Loan Association has approved your application for a $40,000 mortgage. The only trouble is that they want to issue a 25-year, 9% variable rate mortgage instead of the 30-year, fixed-rate loan that you would rather have. If mortgage rates go to 9½% right *after* you sign the papers, how long will it be before you own the house free of the mortgage? (The mortgage is so arranged that an increase in interest rates will not increase the size of the mortgage payments, but will increase the duration of the mortgage. You won't pay more per year, you'll just pay longer.)

To simplify some of the computation, assume that you were able to secure a mortgage such that the payments are made annually at the end of each year.

Solution:

First of all, let's find the size of the annual mortgage payment with equation (8-1) and the annuity factor for 9%, 25 periods.

$$\text{annuity} = \frac{S_0}{\text{pvaf}}$$

$$= \frac{\$40,000}{9.8226} = \$4072.24$$

So, our mortgage payment will be $4072.24 each year. Since the size of the annual payments will remain constant, the additional interest must be paid by increasing the number of payments, on the duration of the annuity. With a new interest rate of 9½%, how many annual payments of $4072.24 must we make so that the mortgage will still have a present value of $40,000? Well, since we know the size of the annuity and its present value when discounted at 9½%, we can find the annuity factor and then go to the table to find its duration:

$$\text{pvaf} = \frac{S_0}{\text{annuity}}$$

$$= \frac{\$40,000}{\$4072.24} = 9.8226.$$

If we turn to the table, we find 9.8226 between the 29th and 30th periods. The increase in the interest rate caused your mortgage to stretch out to accomodate the extra interest that must be paid. Now you can see why the savings and loan did *not* grant your request for a 30-year mortgage—they are restricted by law from granting mortgages in excess of 30 years. If they want to issue mortgages with variable interest rates, they must issue 20- or 25-year mortgages instead so that these mortgages will have room to expand.

Our next problem is relatively simple. We have to choose between two competing investment projects and, as you might guess, the duration of the annuity will play an important part in our decision.

Problem 8-8:

In 1975 a small town north of Fort Worth, Texas was negotiating with a solar energy firm in Nevada for the installation of a solar power system. This would consist of 170,000 square feet of coated copper heat absorber plates covered with tempered glass that would be used to heat water to power four low-order thermal engines. The engines would drive existing generators to produce four megawatts for consumption by the town. Hot water storage tanks would permit full load operation for almost 100 hours without sunlight.

Construction costs for the solar plant would amount to $1000 per kilowatt while a conventional oil-fired plant would cost $450 per kilowatt. In addition, the solar plant would require a total annual expenditure of $50,000 for maintenance for the duration of its 30-year expected life, while the oil-fired plant would require $450,000 annually when run at expected loads. If the town plans to finance the power plant with a new issue of 6½% municipal bonds, how long would the solar plant have to last in order to make it the more economical choice?

Solution:

The solar plant costs $2,200,000 more, but will have annual operating costs of $400,000 less than the oil-fired plant. The question can now be phrased this way: how many years must the town realize the $400,000 annual savings before the solar plant becomes the cheaper alternative?

You *cannot* simply divide the additional cost of the solar plant by the annual savings in order to find the number of years the plant must last. Each $400,000 annual savings occurs in the future and must be discounted back to the present before a comparison can be made. Since the saving is an equal amount every year, and hence an annuity, we can use expression (8-2) and our table to compute our answer:

$$\text{pvaf} = \frac{S_0}{\text{annuity}}$$

$$= \frac{\$2,200,000}{\$400,000} = 5.5000.$$

If we go to the table and look *down* the 6½% column, we will find a factor of 5.4845 in the 7th period and 6.0888 in the 8th. We conclude that the solar plant would have to last slightly more than seven years in order for it to be the preferred alternative. It in fact had an expected life of around 30 years.

Suppose that you decided to use the payback period method instead of the technique above, what would the answer be in that case? Well, $2,200,000 initial cost divided by the $400,000 annual savings gives us a payback period of 5½ years. According to the payback period, the additional cost would be *recovered* in 5½ years, but this ignores the time value of money. Unless money has a zero alternative cost to you, the payback period is not the method to use.

Let's now take a look at a little retirement problem:

Problem 8-9:

Prior to 1972, any soldier who died during retirement left his surviving spouse with no retirement benefits (payment ceased with his death). In 1972, however, the Army and the other uniformed services began offering an alternative to this system. This alternative allowed the surviving spouse to continue to draw up to 55% of the retirement pay in exchange for surrendering 2½% of the first $3600 retirement pay and 10% of the remainder during the time the veteran was drawing his pension. If the veteran dies, the survivor would receive all 55% of the retired pay until age 62, after that the survivor's benefit would be reduced by the amount of Social Security paid to the surviving spouse.

If a lieutenant colonel retired in 1972 with 20 years of service, he would draw about $9144 each year for the rest of his life. In order to provide survivor's benefits for his wife he would have to surrender annually:

$$(2\tfrac{1}{2}\%) \ (\$3600) \ = \ \$ \ 90.00$$
$$(10\%) \ (\$5544) \ = \ \underline{\$554.40}$$
$$\$644.40$$

Of course, the colonel could decide to skip the survivor's benefit plan and put the $644.40 in a savings account at 5% compounded annually. If the colonel was 42 years old at retirement and expected to live until 70, and if his wife was 38 years old and expected to draw $2400 annually from Social Security when she turned 62, how long would *she* have to live to justify the election of the survivor's benefit plan?

Solution:

We can see that we have payments going out for one period and payments coming in for another, so the question is really this: how long must the second stream of payments be received if its present value is to be equal to the present value of the payments surrendered? (It might help to refer to Figure 8-2 while we solve the problems.)

We'll start with the payments surrendered. If $644.40 is surrendered annually for 28 years, then the value of these payments, discounted at 5%, when the colonel is age 42 (we'll let the subscripts refer to the *age* of the colonel)

$$S_{42} = \text{annuity (pvaf)}$$

$$= \$644.40(14.8981) \quad = \$9600.34.$$

This is the value of the payments at the beginning of the annuity when the colonel retires. But, when the colonel dies 28 years later at age 70, it will have a value of

$$S_{70} = \frac{S_{42}}{\text{pvf}}$$

$$= \frac{\$9600.34}{.2551} \quad = \$37,633.63.$$

$37,633.63 will be the value of the costs at the end of the annuity, when the colonel dies at age 70, so how many years must the widow receive her benefits in order for them to have a present value equal to the cost of the plan?

Since the widow's benefits will begin when the colonel is expected to die, and she is already past age 62, her benefits are

$$(55\%)\,(\$9144) \quad = \$5029.20$$
$$\text{less Social Security} \quad = \underline{\$2400.00}$$
$$\$2629.20 \text{ per year.}$$

Now that we have the amount of the annuity benefit, we can use expression (8-2) to find the annuity factor:

$$\text{pvaf} = \frac{S_{70}}{\text{annuity}}$$

$$= \frac{\$37,633.63}{\$2629.20} = 14.3137.$$

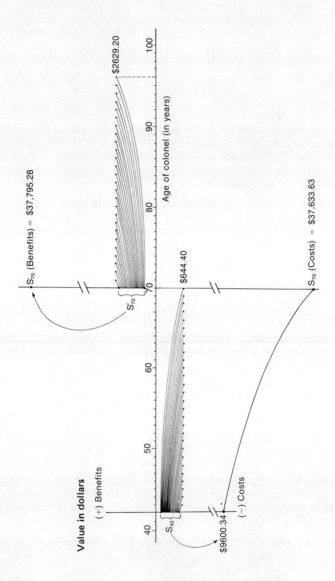

Figure 8-2. Problem 8-9. Finding the duration of an annuity benefit that offsets the present value of an annuity cost.

If we look at the table under 5% we determine that the widow must receive the annuity for almost 26 periods in order for the present value of the $2629.20 annual benefit to exceed the present value of the annual $644.40 expense paid years ago. If she lives 26 years, the value of the benefit the year the colonel dies, S_{70}, will be $2629.20(14.3752), or $37,795.28. The colonel's wife must live 26 years after the colonel's death, or until she is 92 years old, to justify selection of the survivor's benefit plan.

So much for our little retirement problem. Then again, maybe we should say long retirement problem. However, we won't say that it was a *hard* problem because it wasn't. It did have several parts which had to be solved separately, but this is something that should be familiar to you by now.

Our last topic in this chapter deals with the discounted rate of return and we'll take a look at it right now.

THE DISCOUNTED RATE OF RETURN

The discounted rate of return in this chapter is the same as the discounted rate of return we examined earlier in Chapter 5: it is the discount rate that will make the *present value* of an annuity equal to a single payment today.

Again we're going to use the annuity factor equation (8-2) developed in the last section. Instead of going down the discount rate column in the annuity table to find the appropriate period n, as we did in the last section, we'll begin with the period and go across the row until we find the annuity factor under the appropriate discount rate. Let's try a problem and see how this works.

Problem 8-10:

You still want to subscribe to your national magazine and you know that discounting future subscriptions at 5% won't make the lifetime subscription attractive compared to the $8.50 annual subscription cost. Well, what discount rate will make the present value of the annual cost equivalent to the present value of the lifetime rate? (Assume that you still have 50 years left to live.)

Solution:

What discount rate will make a 49-year ordinary annuity plus an initial $8.50 payment worth $200 today? Or, what discount rate will make an ordinary annuity of $8.50 equal to $200-$8.50 or $191.50 today? Well, if we use expression (8-2), we can find the value for the ordinary annuity factor:

$$\text{pvaf} = \frac{S_0}{\text{annuity}}$$

$$= \frac{\$191.50}{\$8.50} = 22.5294.$$

If we look in the annuity table along the 49th period row, we find that 22.5294 is between the factors for 3.5% and 4%. You could interpolate if you care to, but why bother? You know that you can do better on your money elsewhere so you don't want the lifetime subscription.

Since the problem involved a magazine subscription, we had to deal with an annuity due. The problem would have been even easier if it had been an ordinary annuity since we wouldn't have to worry about the initial payment.

Our next problem deals with energy conservation. In fact, it even gave us a little trouble when we wrote it up. It seems that we get the right answer even when we work it wrong.

Problem 8-11:

In early 1976, an article on energy conservation in a leading newspaper discussed the profitability of insulating private homes:

" . . . ceiling insulation in the home costs $300 on the average to install. If the house has an expected lifetime of 25 years, and if the insulation will save about seven barrels of oil each year, the typical homeowner can save 175 barrels of oil. With oil costing around $16 a barrel, the saving over the life of the house will amount to $2800. Given the $300 initial investment and the $2500 saved, you will have a fine return on your investment. . . . "

Given these assumptions, what *is* the return on investment?

Solution:

Well, since we save seven barrels a year at $16 a barrel, that's $112 saved each year. Since our investment is $300, our return is $112/$300 = 37.333% annually, right?

Wrong! We have ignored both the time value of money and the fact that the savings last only 25 years.

Instead, the question should be rephrased: "what discount rate gives a $112, 25-year annuity a present value of $300?" *Now* we can solve the problem:

$$\text{pvaf} = \frac{S_0}{\text{annuity}}$$

$$= \frac{\$300}{\$112} = 2.6786.$$

We go to the table and look across the 25th period row until we find 2.7017 in the 37% column and 2.6307 in the 38% column. If you care to interpolate, this comes to 37.325%, or around 37 1/3%.

Now that's right. But why did we get the right answer when we worked it wrong? Interestingly enough, the discount rate was high enough and the duration long enough for the problem to be treated as a perpetual annuity.

Speaking of perpetual annuities, we should return to the topic for a moment and see how a rate of return problem might be solved. In the past the British issued a form of perpetual bonds called Consols. Let's look at one:

Problem 8-12:

Suppose that back in 1776 you paid the British government £85½ to finance the war in the Colonies (you're a Tory). In exchange you were promised a payment of £3 each year thereafter. What is the yield?

Solution:

We know that our table isn't long enough to handle the perpetual annuity, but we know that we can use expression (8-2) to find the annuity factor:

$$\text{pvaf} = \frac{S_0}{\text{annuity}}$$

$$= \frac{£85\frac{1}{2}}{£3} .$$

And, as long as we remember that this is a *perpetual* annuity, then we know that the reciprocal of the annuity factor is the discount rate:

$$r = \frac{1}{\text{pvaf}} = \frac{\text{annuity}}{S_0}$$

$$= \frac{£3}{£85\frac{1}{2}} = 3.51\%$$

This is actually a much simpler problem than finding yield on a bond with a fixed maturity. In this case, a £3 per year payment divided by the £85½ investment gives the actual 3.51% yield on British Consols in 1776, according to Sidney Homer's *A History of Interest Rates.*

That problem may have been simple, but let's see what happens when we return to the topic of mortgage valuation one more time.

In the midst of the Real Estate Investment Trust (REIT) panic of 1974-1975, a leading financial weekly carried an article on an investment company that specialized in picking up foreclosed properties from troubled REITs at a discount. The discount, however, was not generally in the form of a lower sale price because a REIT that bought a piece of property for one price and sold it for a lower one would have a realized loss. That doesn't look good on the books in a good year, much less in a bad year. To avoid this problem, the REIT would sell the property to the investment company close to the old higher price, and then take back a mortgage at below market interest rates on the property it just sold. The fact that the investment company paid, for example, 6½% interest on the mortgage instead of 9% served as its discount. That might work out to be the same loss for the REIT selling the property, but the loss would be easier to disguise.

Problem 8-13:

One such transaction involved a property that a REIT had purchased for $14 million and whose market value had deteriorated to $10 million. The REIT needed cash rather badly and wanted to sell the property and yet avoid the entry of a $4 million loss on its books. If the REIT wanted $3 million in cash and would take back a 20-year level payment mortgage on the remaining $11 million, what interest rate would it have to offer the investment company to make a $10 million piece of property appear to be worth $14 million? (At the time of the transaction, comparable mortgages were yielding around 9% annually.)

Solution:

Remember that the value of a mortgage depends on the present value of the future payments. The annuity is what is valued in a mortgage and the present value of the annuity will be different for every discount rate.

The $3 million cash payment has a present value of $3 million, so the recovery of the $4 million loss that the REIT *doesn't* want on the books has to be done by making the $11 million mortgage worth $4 million less (or $7 million) to the investment company buying the property. In other words, the annual payment for 20 years that will amortize a $7 million mortgage at 9% (the actual present value and market discount rate), must *also* amortize an $11 million mortgage at some unknown discount rate. First let's find the size of the annuity payment, then we'll find the unknown discount rate. If the annuity factor for 9%, 20 periods, is 9.1285, then the annuity is

$$\text{annuity} = \frac{S_0}{\text{pvaf}}$$

$$= \frac{\$7,000,000}{9.1285} = \$766,829.16.$$

If an annual payment of $766,829.16 for 20 years will amortize a $7 million mortgage at 9%, then what discount rate will make the same $766,821 annual payment amortize an $11 million mortgage? Well, we have the annual payment and the present value of *all* the annual payments, so let's compute the ratio:

$$\text{pvaf} = \frac{S_0}{\text{annuity}}$$

$$= \frac{\$11,000,000}{\$766,829.16} = 14.3448.$$

This is the annuity factor we find in the 20th period row between 3% and 3½%. If we interpolate, we will find that a 3.4% discount rate will give a $766,829.16, 20-year annuity a present value of $11 million.

Now the REIT can sell the depreciated property to the investment company and disguise the $4 million loss on its books. The property is sold to the investment company for $14 million—$3 million in cash and the remainder in a $766,829.16, 20-year annuity carrying a 3.4% rate of return. Since the annuity has a present value of $11 million when discounted at 3.4%, the REIT shows no loss on its books.

On the other hand, the investment company has commmitted itself to pay $766,829.16, for the next 20 years. Since this future expenditure stream has a present cost of $7 million (discounted at 9%), the company really only pays $3 million plus $7 million, or $10 million for the property.

Will this loss get noticed in the annual report? It depends on whether or not anyone notices that the REIT is buying mortgages at 3.4% when the actual market rate is *much* higher.

In the next problem, we are going to look for the rate of return on an investment, a rather large investment.

Problem 8-14:

The Physics Department of a major eastern university recently researched the financial feasibility of establishing colonies in space. The tremendous initial cost would be repaid by having the colonies collect solar energy for microwave transmission to the Earth, eventually supplying the bulk of Earth's energy needs. The construction of the initial colony would make extensive use of material mined on the moon to avoid the expensive necessity of lifting everything from Earth. This colony would be self-sustaining, with the capability of building additional colonies using almost no material from Earth. Finally, it was estimated that 16 colonies could produce all the energy the Earth would want at the expected price.

The project would incur a cost of roughly $20 billion each year for 17 years and after that return roughly $50 billion forever. What is the discounted rate of return on this project?

Solution:

We have costs and benefits occurring in different time periods, so we must find a discount rate that will reduce each to equivalent present values. Since we have two future annuities, we could resort to our trial and error method again.

It doesn't matter where we start, but let's try 10% and find the present value of the costs.

$$S_0 = \text{annuity (pvaf)}$$

$$= \$20 \text{ billion}(8.0216) = \$160.4 \text{ billion}.$$

As for the forever annuity of $50 billion, we use the perpetual annuity discount formula:

$$S_{17} = \frac{\text{annuity}}{r}$$

$$= \frac{\$50 \text{ billion}}{10\%} = \$500 \text{ billion.}$$

But this annuity begins 17 years later, so it must be discounted back to the present to make it comparable with the present value of the costs.

$$S_0 = S_{17}(\text{pvf})$$

$$= \$500 \text{ billion}(.1978) = \$98.9 \text{ billion}$$

Since the present value of the costs ($160.4 billion) exceeds the present value of the benefits ($98.9 billion), we'll have to change the discount rate and try again.

After MUCH trial and error, we've narrowed it down to between 8% (where the costs have a present value of $182.4 billion and the revenues a value of $168.9 billion) and 7½% ($188.68 billion and $195.0 billion, respectively).

We could interpolate, or we could take another guess somewhere between these limits and interpolate over a smaller range, but you get the idea.

This concludes our discussion of the discounted rate of return. As you can see, the problems in this section were similar to problems we've faced earlier, even those problems that tend to be long can be easily solved if they are broken into their component parts before the solution begins.

SUMMARY

In this chapter, we examined three additional annuity topics: the amount of annuity, the duration of annuity, and the discounted rate of return. The methodology employed in this chapter is similar to that used in earlier chapters: given values for any three of the four variables in an annuity problem, the remaining value can always be found.

We began our discussion with problems involving the amount or size of the annuity. Finding the amount of annuity was only a matter of rearranging the present value of annuity formula (7-1) in such a way as to derive our amount of annuity formula (8-1) below:

$$\text{annuity} = \frac{S_0}{\text{pvaf}}$$

When we came to the topic of the duration of the annuity, we further rearranged expression (7-1) to yield our annuity factor equation (8-2) below:

$$\text{pvaf} = \frac{S_0}{\text{annuity}}$$

Whenever we were seeking the duration of the annuity, we simply used the information in the problem to compute the factor, and then went *down* the discount rate column until we found the value for n, the duration of the annuity.

Problems involving the discounted rate of return were also solved with the help of the annuity factor equation above. This time, however, we started with the duration of the annuity and went across the table until we found the appropriate discount rate. The only difficult discounted rate of return problem we attempted was the last, which involved two future annuities. When we attempted to find the discount rate that would reduce each to equivalent present values, we simply resorted to the trial and error method and experimented until we got close enough for interpolation.

As we close this chapter, we want to offer a comment on the construction and use of the annuity table. Throughout the course of this text, we have argued that it is necessary to understand the construction of the table before you begin to use it. Not only does this help you better understand the way in which it should be used, it also helps you when the table doesn't have enough discount rates, or periods. In short, if you know how the table is constructed, then you should also know how to lengthen or otherwise expand the table to suit your needs.

After solving some of the problems in this chapter as well as the problems in Chapters 5 and 6, you'll understand why we made the present value and the annuity tables as extensive as we did. It's simply easier to search for a discount rate or a value for n if the table is not overly abbreviated, and it also means that you won't have to interpolate as often.

ADDITIONAL PROBLEMS

1.   Your kid brother recently dropped out of college because he ran short of money in his second semester. Older but wiser, he has decided to manage his money differently this time. How can he budget the meager $3000 he has managed to save so that it will last him the 3 remaining years until graduation? He currently keeps the money in a 6% savings account which compounds interest monthly and he wants to know how much he can withdraw monthly.

Answer: $91.27

2. Seven years ago you bought a house with a $10,000, 8½% mortgage amortized over 30 years. You are filling out your tax forms and want to deduct the interest part of your payment. How much interest did you pay last year if your mortgage payments were made annually? (Hint: there are 23 remaining payments on the mortgage.)

    Answer: $799.12

3. It just happens that your request for a $45,000, 30-year, 9% mortgage has been approved and that that the monthly payment will amount to $362.08. (Interest on the mortgage is compounded monthly, so the amount of annuity is based on a .75% rate for 360 periods.) If you suspect that mortgage rates will go down by ½% during the next few months, what will be the size of the annuity payment if you wait until you can obtain the same mortgage at 8½%? (Hint: set your calculator for floating decimal and use the pvaf equation on page 106 to find the annuity factor.)

    Answer: $346.01

4. If our colonel (Problem 8-9) dies at 60 instead of 70, how old would his wife be when the present value of the benefits equaled the present value of the costs of the option?

    Answer: a little over 60

5. Albert Gallatin's 1809 report on the First Bank of the United States describes the 1791 subscription by the U.S. government to 5000 (or 20%) of the capital shares of the bank for $2,000,000, which was to be paid in 10 equal annual installments of $200,000. The government later sold 2493 shares in 1796 for $1,246,500; 287 shares in 1797 for $137,760; and the remaining 2220 shares in 1802 for $1,287,600. Exclusive of dividends, what rate of return did the U.S. government get on its bank investment if the government made its first payment in 1791? (What discount rate will make the present value of the money paid out equal to the present value of the money received for the sale of its shares?)

    Answer: 8.82%

6. In 1975, a well-known department store in Allentown, Pennsylvania offered a "Christmas Club Bonus Plan" in which Christmas Club checks could be turned into store purchase certificates 5% larger than the checks. If you put $100 into your club account at the end of each month for 11 months and bought purchase certificates at the end of the twelfth month, what was your monthly rate of return on club account deposits?

Answer: .81%

APPENDIX

TABLE A-1. PRESENT VALUE FACTORS

PERIOD	0.0%	.5%	1.0%	1.5%	2.0%	2.5%	3.0%	PERIOD
1	1.0000	.9950	.9901	.9852	.9804	.9756	.9709	1
2	1.0000	.9901	.9803	.9707	.9612	.9518	.9426	2
3	1.0000	.9851	.9706	.9563	.9423	.9286	.9151	3
4	1.0000	.9802	.9610	.9422	.9238	.9060	.8885	4
5	1.0000	.9754	.9515	.9283	.9057	.8839	.8626	5
6	1.0000	.9705	.9420	.9145	.8880	.8623	.8375	6
7	1.0000	.9657	.9327	.9010	.8706	.8413	.8131	7
8	1.0000	.9609	.9235	.8877	.8535	.8207	.7894	8
9	1.0000	.9561	.9143	.8746	.8368	.8007	.7664	9
10	1.0000	.9513	.9053	.8617	.8203	.7812	.7441	10
11	1.0000	.9466	.8963	.8489	.8043	.7621	.7224	11
12	1.0000	.9419	.8874	.8364	.7885	.7436	.7014	12
13	1.0000	.9372	.8787	.8240	.7730	.7254	.6810	13
14	1.0000	.9326	.8700	.8118	.7579	.7077	.6611	14
15	1.0000	.9279	.8613	.7999	.7430	.6905	.6419	15
16	1.0000	.9233	.8528	.7880	.7284	.6736	.6232	16
17	1.0000	.9187	.8444	.7764	.7142	.6572	.6050	17
18	1.0000	.9141	.8360	.7649	.7002	.6412	.5874	18
19	1.0000	.9096	.8277	.7536	.6864	.6255	.5703	19
20	1.0000	.9051	.8195	.7425	.6730	.6103	.5537	20
21	1.0000	.9006	.8114	.7315	.6598	.5954	.5375	21
22	1.0000	.8961	.8034	.7207	.6468	.5809	.5219	22
23	1.0000	.8916	.7954	.7100	.6342	.5667	.5067	23
24	1.0000	.8872	.7876	.6995	.6217	.5529	.4919	24
25	1.0000	.8828	.7798	.6892	.6095	.5394	.4776	25
26	1.0000	.8784	.7720	.6790	.5976	.5262	.4637	26
27	1.0000	.8740	.7644	.6690	.5859	.5134	.4502	27
28	1.0000	.8697	.7568	.6591	.5744	.5009	.4371	28
29	1.0000	.8653	.7493	.6494	.5631	.4887	.4243	29
30	1.0000	.8610	.7419	.6398	.5521	.4767	.4120	30
31	1.0000	.8567	.7346	.6303	.5412	.4651	.4000	31
32	1.0000	.8525	.7273	.6210	.5306	.4538	.3883	32
33	1.0000	.8482	.7201	.6118	.5202	.4427	.3770	33
34	1.0000	.8440	.7130	.6028	.5100	.4319	.3660	34
35	1.0000	.8398	.7059	.5939	.5000	.4214	.3554	35
36	1.0000	.8356	.6989	.5851	.4902	.4111	.3450	36
37	1.0000	.8315	.6920	.5764	.4806	.4011	.3350	37
38	1.0000	.8274	.6852	.5679	.4712	.3913	.3252	38
39	1.0000	.8232	.6784	.5595	.4619	.3817	.3158	39
40	1.0000	.8191	.6717	.5513	.4529	.3724	.3066	40
41	1.0000	.8151	.6650	.5431	.4440	.3633	.2976	41
42	1.0000	.8110	.6584	.5351	.4353	.3545	.2890	42
43	1.0000	.8070	.6519	.5272	.4268	.3458	.2805	43
44	1.0000	.8030	.6454	.5194	.4184	.3374	.2724	44
45	1.0000	.7990	.6391	.5117	.4102	.3292	.2644	45
46	1.0000	.7950	.6327	.5042	.4022	.3211	.2567	46
47	1.0000	.7910	.6265	.4967	.3943	.3133	.2493	47
48	1.0000	.7871	.6203	.4894	.3865	.3057	.2420	48
49	1.0000	.7832	.6141	.4821	.3790	.2982	.2350	49
50	1.0000	.7793	.6080	.4750	.3715	.2909	.2281	50

TABLE A-1. PRESENT VALUE FACTORS (Continued)

PERIOD	3.5%	4.0%	4.5%	5.0%	5.5%	6.0%	6.5%	PERIOD
1	.9662	.9615	.9569	.9524	.9479	.9434	.9390	1
2	.9335	.9246	.9157	.9070	.8985	.8900	.8817	2
3	.9019	.8890	.8763	.8638	.8516	.8396	.8278	3
4	.8714	.8548	.8386	.8227	.8072	.7921	.7773	4
5	.8420	.8219	.8025	.7835	.7651	.7473	.7299	5
6	.8135	.7903	.7679	.7462	.7252	.7050	.6853	6
7	.7860	.7599	.7348	.7107	.6874	.6651	.6435	7
8	.7594	.7307	.7032	.6768	.6516	.6274	.6042	8
9	.7337	.7026	.6729	.6446	.6176	.5919	.5674	9
10	.7089	.6756	.6439	.6139	.5854	.5584	.5327	10
11	.6849	.6496	.6162	.5847	.5549	.5268	.5002	11
12	.6618	.6246	.5897	.5568	.5260	.4970	.4697	12
13	.6394	.6006	.5643	.5303	.4986	.4688	.4410	13
14	.6178	.5775	.5400	.5051	.4726	.4423	.4141	14
15	.5969	.5553	.5167	.4810	.4479	.4173	.3888	15
16	.5767	.5339	.4945	.4581	.4246	.3936	.3651	16
17	.5572	.5134	.4732	.4363	.4024	.3714	.3428	17
18	.5384	.4936	.4528	.4155	.3815	.3503	.3219	18
19	.5202	.4746	.4333	.3957	.3616	.3305	.3022	19
20	.5026	.4564	.4146	.3769	.3427	.3118	.2838	20
21	.4856	.4388	.3968	.3589	.3249	.2942	.2665	21
22	.4692	.4220	.3797	.3418	.3079	.2775	.2502	22
23	.4533	.4057	.3634	.3256	.2919	.2618	.2349	23
24	.4380	.3901	.3477	.3101	.2767	.2470	.2206	24
25	.4231	.3751	.3327	.2953	.2622	.2330	.2071	25
26	.4088	.3607	.3184	.2812	.2486	.2198	.1945	26
27	.3950	.3468	.3047	.2678	.2356	.2074	.1826	27
28	.3817	.3335	.2916	.2551	.2233	.1956	.1715	28
29	.3687	.3207	.2790	.2429	.2117	.1846	.1610	29
30	.3563	.3083	.2670	.2314	.2006	.1741	.1512	30
31	.3442	.2965	.2555	.2204	.1902	.1643	.1420	31
32	.3326	.2851	.2445	.2099	.1803	.1550	.1333	32
33	.3213	.2741	.2340	.1999	.1709	.1462	.1252	33
34	.3105	.2636	.2239	.1904	.1620	.1379	.1175	34
35	.3000	.2534	.2143	.1813	.1535	.1301	.1103	35
36	.2898	.2437	.2050	.1727	.1455	.1227	.1036	36
37	.2800	.2343	.1962	.1644	.1379	.1158	.0973	37
38	.2706	.2253	.1878	.1566	.1307	.1092	.0914	38
39	.2614	.2166	.1797	.1491	.1239	.1031	.0858	39
40	.2526	.2083	.1719	.1420	.1175	.0972	.0805	40
41	.2440	.2003	.1645	.1353	.1113	.0917	.0756	41
42	.2358	.1926	.1574	.1288	.1055	.0865	.0710	42
43	.2278	.1852	.1507	.1227	.1000	.0816	.0667	43
44	.2201	.1780	.1442	.1169	.0948	.0770	.0626	44
45	.2127	.1712	.1380	.1113	.0899	.0727	.0588	45
46	.2055	.1646	.1320	.1060	.0852	.0685	.0552	46
47	.1985	.1583	.1263	.1009	.0807	.0647	.0518	47
48	.1918	.1522	.1209	.0961	.0765	.0610	.0487	48
49	.1853	.1463	.1157	.0916	.0725	.0575	.0457	49
50	.1791	.1407	.1107	.0872	.0688	.0543	.0429	50

TABLE A-1. PRESENT VALUE FACTORS (Continued)

PERIOD	7.0%	7.5%	8.0%	8.5%	9.0%	9.5%	10.0%	PERIOD
1	.9346	.9302	.9259	.9217	.9174	.9132	.9091	1
2	.8734	.8653	.8573	.8495	.8417	.8340	.8264	2
3	.8163	.8050	.7938	.7829	.7722	.7617	.7513	3
4	.7629	.7488	.7350	.7216	.7084	.6956	.6830	4
5	.7130	.6966	.6806	.6650	.6499	.6352	.6209	5
6	.6663	.6480	.6302	.6129	.5963	.5801	.5645	6
7	.6227	.6028	.5835	.5649	.5470	.5298	.5132	7
8	.5820	.5607	.5403	.5207	.5019	.4838	.4665	8
9	.5439	.5216	.5002	.4799	.4604	.4418	.4241	9
10	.5083	.4852	.4632	.4423	.4224	.4035	.3855	10
11	.4751	.4513	.4289	.4076	.3875	.3685	.3505	11
12	.4440	.4199	.3971	.3757	.3555	.3365	.3186	12
13	.4150	.3906	.3677	.3463	.3262	.3073	.2897	13
14	.3878	.3633	.3405	.3191	.2992	.2807	.2633	14
15	.3624	.3380	.3152	.2941	.2745	.2563	.2394	15
16	.3387	.3144	.2919	.2711	.2519	.2341	.2176	16
17	.3166	.2925	.2703	.2499	.2311	.2138	.1978	17
18	.2959	.2720	.2502	.2303	.2120	.1952	.1799	18
19	.2765	.2531	.2317	.2122	.1945	.1783	.1635	19
20	.2584	.2354	.2145	.1956	.1784	.1628	.1486	20
21	.2415	.2190	.1987	.1803	.1637	.1487	.1351	21
22	.2257	.2037	.1839	.1662	.1502	.1358	.1228	22
23	.2109	.1895	.1703	.1531	.1378	.1240	.1117	23
24	.1971	.1763	.1577	.1412	.1264	.1133	.1015	24
25	.1842	.1640	.1460	.1301	.1160	.1034	.0923	25
26	.1722	.1525	.1352	.1199	.1064	.0945	.0839	26
27	.1609	.1419	.1252	.1105	.0976	.0863	.0763	27
28	.1504	.1320	.1159	.1019	.0895	.0788	.0693	28
29	.1406	.1228	.1073	.0939	.0822	.0719	.0630	29
30	.1314	.1142	.0994	.0865	.0754	.0657	.0573	30
31	.1228	.1063	.0920	.0797	.0691	.0600	.0521	31
32	.1147	.0988	.0852	.0735	.0634	.0548	.0474	32
33	.1072	.0919	.0789	.0677	.0582	.0500	.0431	33
34	.1002	.0855	.0730	.0624	.0534	.0457	.0391	34
35	.0937	.0796	.0676	.0575	.0490	.0417	.0356	35
36	.0875	.0740	.0626	.0530	.0449	.0381	.0323	36
37	.0818	.0688	.0580	.0489	.0412	.0348	.0294	37
38	.0765	.0640	.0537	.0450	.0378	.0318	.0267	38
39	.0715	.0596	.0497	.0415	.0347	.0290	.0243	39
40	.0668	.0554	.0460	.0383	.0318	.0265	.0221	40
41	.0624	.0516	.0426	.0353	.0292	.0242	.0201	41
42	.0583	.0480	.0395	.0325	.0268	.0221	.0183	42
43	.0545	.0446	.0365	.0300	.0246	.0202	.0166	43
44	.0509	.0415	.0338	.0276	.0226	.0184	.0151	44
45	.0476	.0386	.0313	.0254	.0207	.0168	.0137	45
46	.0445	.0359	.0290	.0235	.0190	.0154	.0125	46
47	.0416	.0334	.0269	.0216	.0174	.0140	.0113	47
48	.0389	.0311	.0249	.0199	.0160	.0128	.0103	48
49	.0363	.0289	.0230	.0184	.0147	.0117	.0094	49
50	.0339	.0269	.0213	.0169	.0134	.0107	.0085	50

TABLE A-1. PRESENT VALUE FACTORS (Continued)

PERIOD	10.5%	11.0%	11.5%	12.0%	12.5%	13.0%	13.5%	PERIOD
1	.9050	.9009	.8969	.8929	.8889	.8850	.8811	1
2	.8190	.8116	.8044	.7972	.7901	.7831	.7763	2
3	.7412	.7312	.7214	.7118	.7023	.6931	.6839	3
4	.6707	.6587	.6470	.6355	.6243	.6133	.6026	4
5	.6070	.5935	.5803	.5674	.5549	.5428	.5309	5
6	.5493	.5346	.5204	.5066	.4933	.4803	.4678	6
7	.4971	.4817	.4667	.4523	.4385	.4251	.4121	7
8	.4499	.4339	.4186	.4039	.3897	.3762	.3631	8
9	.4071	.3909	.3754	.3606	.3464	.3329	.3199	9
10	.3684	.3522	.3367	.3220	.3079	.2946	.2819	10
11	.3334	.3173	.3020	.2875	.2737	.2607	.2483	11
12	.3018	.2858	.2708	.2567	.2433	.2307	.2188	12
13	.2731	.2575	.2429	.2292	.2163	.2042	.1928	13
14	.2471	.2320	.2178	.2046	.1922	.1807	.1698	14
15	.2236	.2090	.1954	.1827	.1709	.1599	.1496	15
16	.2024	.1883	.1752	.1631	.1519	.1415	.1318	16
17	.1832	.1696	.1572	.1456	.1350	.1252	.1162	17
18	.1658	.1528	.1409	.1300	.1200	.1108	.1023	18
19	.1500	.1377	.1264	.1161	.1067	.0981	.0902	19
20	.1358	.1240	.1134	.1037	.0948	.0868	.0794	20
21	.1229	.1117	.1017	.0926	.0843	.0768	.0700	21
22	.1112	.1007	.0912	.0826	.0749	.0680	.0617	22
23	.1006	.0907	.0818	.0738	.0666	.0601	.0543	23
24	.0911	.0817	.0734	.0659	.0592	.0532	.0479	24
25	.0824	.0736	.0658	.0588	.0526	.0471	.0422	25
26	.0746	.0663	.0590	.0525	.0468	.0417	.0372	26
27	.0675	.0597	.0529	.0469	.0416	.0369	.0327	27
28	.0611	.0538	.0475	.0419	.0370	.0326	.0288	28
29	.0553	.0485	.0426	.0374	.0329	.0289	.0254	29
30	.0500	.0437	.0382	.0334	.0292	.0256	.0224	30
31	.0453	.0394	.0342	.0298	.0260	.0226	.0197	31
32	.0410	.0355	.0307	.0266	.0231	.0200	.0174	32
33	.0371	.0319	.0275	.0238	.0205	.0177	.0153	33
34	.0335	.0288	.0247	.0212	.0182	.0157	.0135	34
35	.0304	.0259	.0222	.0189	.0162	.0139	.0119	35
36	.0275	.0234	.0199	.0169	.0144	.0123	.0105	36
37	.0249	.0210	.0178	.0151	.0128	.0109	.0092	37
38	.0225	.0190	.0160	.0135	.0114	.0096	.0081	38
39	.0204	.0171	.0143	.0120	.0101	.0085	.0072	39
40	.0184	.0154	.0129	.0107	.0090	.0075	.0063	40
41	.0167	.0139	.0115	.0096	.0080	.0067	.0056	41
42	.0151	.0125	.0103	.0086	.0071	.0059	.0049	42
43	.0137	.0112	.0093	.0076	.0063	.0052	.0043	43
44	.0124	.0101	.0083	.0068	.0056	.0046	.0038	44
45	.0112	.0091	.0075	.0061	.0050	.0041	.0034	45
46	.0101	.0082	.0067	.0054	.0044	.0036	.0030	46
47	.0092	.0074	.0060	.0049	.0039	.0032	.0026	47
48	.0083	.0067	.0054	.0043	.0035	.0028	.0023	48
49	.0075	.0060	.0048	.0039	.0031	.0025	.0020	49
50	.0068	.0054	.0043	.0035	.0028	.0022	.0018	50

TABLE A-1. PRESENT VALUE FACTORS (Continued)

PERIOD	14.0%	14.5%	15.0%	15.5%	16.0%	16.5%	17.0%	PERIOD
1	.8772	.8734	.8696	.8658	.8621	.8584	.8547	1
2	.7695	.7628	.7561	.7496	.7432	.7368	.7305	2
3	.6750	.6662	.6575	.6490	.6407	.6324	.6244	3
4	.5921	.5818	.5718	.5619	.5523	.5429	.5337	4
5	.5194	.5081	.4972	.4865	.4761	.4660	.4561	5
6	.4556	.4438	.4323	.4212	.4104	.4000	.3898	6
7	.3996	.3876	.3759	.3647	.3538	.3433	.3332	7
8	.3506	.3385	.3269	.3158	.3050	.2947	.2848	8
9	.3075	.2956	.2843	.2734	.2630	.2530	.2434	9
10	.2697	.2582	.2472	.2367	.2267	.2171	.2080	10
11	.2366	.2255	.2149	.2049	.1954	.1864	.1778	11
12	.2076	.1969	.1869	.1774	.1685	.1600	.1520	12
13	.1821	.1720	.1625	.1536	.1452	.1373	.1299	13
14	.1597	.1502	.1413	.1330	.1252	.1179	.1110	14
15	.1401	.1312	.1229	.1152	.1079	.1012	.0949	15
16	.1229	.1146	.1069	.0997	.0930	.0869	.0811	16
17	.1078	.1001	.0929	.0863	.0802	.0746	.0693	17
18	.0946	.0874	.0808	.0747	.0691	.0640	.0592	18
19	.0829	.0763	.0703	.0647	.0596	.0549	.0506	19
20	.0728	.0667	.0611	.0560	.0514	.0471	.0433	20
21	.0638	.0582	.0531	.0485	.0443	.0405	.0370	21
22	.0560	.0508	.0462	.0420	.0382	.0347	.0316	22
23	.0491	.0444	.0402	.0364	.0329	.0298	.0270	23
24	.0431	.0388	.0349	.0315	.0284	.0256	.0231	24
25	.0378	.0339	.0304	.0273	.0245	.0220	.0197	25
26	.0331	.0296	.0264	.0236	.0211	.0189	.0169	26
27	.0291	.0258	.0230	.0204	.0182	.0162	.0144	27
28	.0255	.0226	.0200	.0177	.0157	.0139	.0123	28
29	.0224	.0197	.0174	.0153	.0135	.0119	.0105	29
30	.0196	.0172	.0151	.0133	.0116	.0102	.0090	30
31	.0172	.0150	.0131	.0115	.0100	.0088	.0077	31
32	.0151	.0131	.0114	.0099	.0087	.0075	.0066	32
33	.0132	.0115	.0099	.0086	.0075	.0065	.0056	33
34	.0116	.0100	.0086	.0075	.0064	.0056	.0048	34
35	.0102	.0087	.0075	.0065	.0055	.0048	.0041	35
36	.0089	.0076	.0065	.0056	.0048	.0041	.0035	36
37	.0078	.0067	.0057	.0048	.0041	.0035	.0030	37
38	.0069	.0058	.0049	.0042	.0036	.0030	.0026	38
39	.0060	.0051	.0043	.0036	.0031	.0026	.0022	39
40	.0053	.0044	.0037	.0031	.0026	.0022	.0019	40
41	.0046	.0039	.0032	.0027	.0023	.0019	.0016	41
42	.0041	.0034	.0028	.0024	.0020	.0016	.0014	42
43	.0036	.0030	.0025	.0020	.0017	.0014	.0012	43
44	.0031	.0026	.0021	.0018	.0015	.0012	.0010	44
45	.0027	.0023	.0019	.0015	.0013	.0010	.0009	45
46	.0024	.0020	.0016	.0013	.0011	.0009	.0007	46
47	.0021	.0017	.0014	.0011	.0009	.0008	.0006	47
48	.0019	.0015	.0012	.0010	.0008	.0007	.0005	48
49	.0016	.0013	.0011	.0009	.0007	.0006	.0005	49
50	.0014	.0011	.0009	.0007	.0006	.0005	.0004	50

TABLE A-1. PRESENT VALUE FACTORS (Continued)

PERIOD	17.5%	18.0%	18.5%	19.0%	20.0%	21.0%	22.0%	PERIOD
1	.8511	.8475	.8439	.8403	.8333	.8264	.8197	1
2	.7243	.7182	.7121	.7062	.6944	.6830	.6719	2
3	.6164	.6086	.6010	.5934	.5787	.5645	.5507	3
4	.5246	.5158	.5071	.4987	.4823	.4665	.4514	4
5	.4465	.4371	.4280	.4190	.4019	.3855	.3700	5
6	.3800	.3704	.3612	.3521	.3349	.3186	.3033	6
7	.3234	.3139	.3048	.2959	.2791	.2633	.2486	7
8	.2752	.2660	.2572	.2487	.2326	.2176	.2038	8
9	.2342	.2255	.2170	.2090	.1938	.1799	.1670	9
10	.1994	.1911	.1832	.1756	.1615	.1486	.1369	10
11	.1697	.1619	.1546	.1476	.1346	.1228	.1122	11
12	.1444	.1372	.1304	.1240	.1122	.1015	.0920	12
13	.1229	.1163	.1101	.1042	.0935	.0839	.0754	13
14	.1046	.0985	.0929	.0876	.0779	.0693	.0618	14
15	.0890	.0835	.0784	.0736	.0649	.0573	.0507	15
16	.0758	.0708	.0661	.0618	.0541	.0474	.0415	16
17	.0645	.0600	.0558	.0520	.0451	.0391	.0340	17
18	.0549	.0508	.0471	.0437	.0376	.0323	.0279	18
19	.0467	.0431	.0398	.0367	.0313	.0267	.0229	19
20	.0397	.0365	.0335	.0308	.0261	.0221	.0187	20
21	.0338	.0309	.0283	.0259	.0217	.0183	.0154	21
22	.0288	.0262	.0239	.0218	.0181	.0151	.0126	22
23	.0245	.0222	.0202	.0183	.0151	.0125	.0103	23
24	.0208	.0188	.0170	.0154	.0126	.0103	.0085	24
25	.0177	.0160	.0144	.0129	.0105	.0085	.0069	25
26	.0151	.0135	.0121	.0109	.0087	.0070	.0057	26
27	.0129	.0115	.0102	.0091	.0073	.0058	.0047	27
28	.0109	.0097	.0086	.0077	.0061	.0048	.0038	28
29	.0093	.0082	.0073	.0064	.0051	.0040	.0031	29
30	.0079	.0070	.0061	.0054	.0042	.0033	.0026	30
31	.0067	.0059	.0052	.0046	.0035	.0027	.0021	31
32	.0057	.0050	.0044	.0038	.0029	.0022	.0017	32
33	.0049	.0042	.0037	.0032	.0024	.0019	.0014	33
34	.0042	.0036	.0031	.0027	.0020	.0015	.0012	34
35	.0035	.0030	.0026	.0023	.0017	.0013	.0009	35
36	.0030	.0026	.0022	.0019	.0014	.0010	.0008	36
37	.0026	.0022	.0019	.0016	.0012	.0009	.0006	37
38	.0022	.0019	.0016	.0013	.0010	.0007	.0005	38
39	.0019	.0016	.0013	.0011	.0008	.0006	.0004	39
40	.0016	.0013	.0011	.0010	.0007	.0005	.0004	40
41	.0013	.0011	.0009	.0008	.0006	.0004	.0003	41
42	.0011	.0010	.0008	.0007	.0005	.0003	.0002	42
43	.0010	.0008	.0007	.0006	.0004	.0003	.0002	43
44	.0008	.0007	.0006	.0005	.0003	.0002	.0002	44
45	.0007	.0006	.0005	.0004	.0003	.0002	.0001	45
46	.0006	.0005	.0004	.0003	.0002	.0002	.0001	46
47	.0005	.0004	.0003	.0003	.0002	.0001	.0001	47
48	.0004	.0004	.0003	.0002	.0002	.0001	.0001	48
49	.0004	.0003	.0002	.0002	.0001	.0001	.0001	49
50	.0003	.0003	.0002	.0002	.0001	.0001	.0000	50

TABLE A-1. PRESENT VALUE FACTORS (Continued) ·

PERIOD	23.0%	24.0%	25.0%	26.0%	27.0%	28.0%	29.0%	PERIOD
1	.8130	.8065	.8000	.7937	.7874	.7813	.7752	1
2	.6610	.6504	.6400	.6299	.6200	.6104	.6009	2
3	.5374	.5245	.5120	.4999	.4882	.4768	.4658	3
4	.4369	.4230	.4096	.3968	.3844	.3725	.3611	4
5	.3552	.3411	.3277	.3149	.3027	.2910	.2799	5
6	.2888	.2751	.2621	.2499	.2383	.2274	.2170	6
7	.2348	.2218	.2097	.1983	.1877	.1776	.1682	7
8	.1909	.1789	.1678	.1574	.1478	.1388	.1304	8
9	.1552	.1443	.1342	.1249	.1164	.1084	.1011	9
10	.1262	.1164	.1074	.0992	.0916	.0847	.0784	10
11	.1026	.0938	.0859	.0787	.0721	.0662	.0607	11
12	.0834	.0757	.0687	.0625	.0568	.0517	.0471	12
13	.0678	.0610	.0550	.0496	.0447	.0404	.0365	13
14	.0551	.0492	.0440	.0393	.0352	.0316	.0283	14
15	.0448	.0397	.0352	.0312	.0277	.0247	.0219	15
16	.0364	.0320	.0281	.0248	.0218	.0193	.0170	16
17	.0296	.0258	.0225	.0197	.0172	.0150	.0132	17
18	.0241	.0208	.0180	.0156	.0135	.0118	.0102	18
19	.0196	.0168	.0144	.0124	.0107	.0092	.0079	19
20	.0159	.0135	.0115	.0098	.0084	.0072	.0061	20
21	.0129	.0109	.0092	.0078	.0066	.0056	.0048	21
22	.0105	.0088	.0074	.0062	.0052	.0044	.0037	22
23	.0086	.0071	.0059	.0049	.0041	.0034	.0029	23
24	.0070	.0057	.0047	.0039	.0032	.0027	.0022	24
25	.0057	.0046	.0038	.0031	.0025	.0021	.0017	25
26	.0046	.0037	.0030	.0025	.0020	.0016	.0013	26
27	.0037	.0030	.0024	.0019	.0016	.0013	.0010	27
28	.0030	.0024	.0019	.0015	.0012	.0010	.0008	28
29	.0025	.0020	.0015	.0012	.0010	.0008	.0006	29
30	.0020	.0016	.0012	.0010	.0008	.0006	.0005	30
31	.0016	.0013	.0010	.0008	.0006	.0005	.0004	31
32	.0013	.0010	.0008	.0006	.0005	.0004	.0003	32
33	.0011	.0008	.0006	.0005	.0004	.0003	.0002	33
34	.0009	.0007	.0005	.0004	.0003	.0002	.0002	34
35	.0007	.0005	.0004	.0003	.0002	.0002	.0001	35
36	.0006	.0004	.0003	.0002	.0002	.0001	.0001	36
37	.0005	.0003	.0003	.0002	.0001	.0001	.0001	37
38	.0004	.0003	.0002	.0002	.0001	.0001	.0001	38
39	.0003	.0002	.0002	.0001	.0001	.0001	.0000	39
40	.0003	.0002	.0001	.0001	.0001	.0001	.0000	40
41	.0002	.0001	.0001	.0001	.0001	.0000	.0000	41
42	.0002	.0001	.0001	.0001	.0000	.0000	.0000	42
43	.0001	.0001	.0001	.0000	.0000	.0000	.0000	43
44	.0001	.0001	.0001	.0000	.0000	.0000	.0000	44
45	.0001	.0001	.0000	.0000	.0000	.0000	.0000	45
46	.0001	.0001	.0000	.0000	.0000	.0000	.0000	46
47	.0001	.0000	.0000	.0000	.0000	.0000	.0000	47
48	.0000	.0000	.0000	.0000	.0000	.0000	.0000	48
49	.0000	.0000	.0000	.0000	.0000	.0000	.0000	49
50	.0000	.0000	.0000	.0000	.0000	.0000	.0000	50

TABLE A-1. PRESENT VALUE FACTORS (Continued)

PERIOD	30.0%	31.0%	32.0%	33.0%	34.0%	35.0%	36.0%	PERIOD
1	.7692	.7634	.7576	.7519	.7463	.7407	.7353	1
2	.5917	.5827	.5739	.5653	.5569	.5487	.5407	2
3	.4552	.4448	.4348	.4251	.4156	.4064	.3975	3
4	.3501	.3396	.3294	.3196	.3102	.3011	.2923	4
5	.2693	.2592	.2495	.2403	.2315	.2230	.2149	5
6	.2072	.1979	.1890	.1807	.1727	.1652	.1580	6
7	.1594	.1510	.1432	.1358	.1289	.1224	.1162	7
8	.1226	.1153	.1085	.1021	.0962	.0906	.0854	8
9	.0943	.0880	.0822	.0768	.0718	.0671	.0628	9
10	.0725	.0672	.0623	.0577	.0536	.0497	.0462	10
11	.0558	.0513	.0472	.0434	.0400	.0368	.0340	11
12	.0429	.0392	.0357	.0326	.0298	.0273	.0250	12
13	.0330	.0299	.0271	.0245	.0223	.0202	.0184	13
14	.0254	.0228	.0205	.0185	.0166	.0150	.0135	14
15	.0195	.0174	.0155	.0139	.0124	.0111	.0099	15
16	.0150	.0133	.0118	.0104	.0093	.0082	.0073	16
17	.0116	.0101	.0089	.0078	.0069	.0061	.0054	17
18	.0089	.0077	.0068	.0059	.0052	.0045	.0039	18
19	.0068	.0059	.0051	.0044	.0038	.0033	.0029	19
20	.0053	.0045	.0039	.0033	.0029	.0025	.0021	20
21	.0040	.0034	.0029	.0025	.0021	.0018	.0016	21
22	.0031	.0026	.0022	.0019	.0016	.0014	.0012	22
23	.0024	.0020	.0017	.0014	.0012	.0010	.0008	23
24	.0018	.0015	.0013	.0011	.0009	.0007	.0006	24
25	.0014	.0012	.0010	.0008	.0007	.0006	.0005	25
26	.0011	.0009	.0007	.0006	.0005	.0004	.0003	26
27	.0008	.0007	.0006	.0005	.0004	.0003	.0002	27
28	.0006	.0005	.0004	.0003	.0003	.0002	.0002	28
29	.0005	.0004	.0003	.0003	.0002	.0002	.0001	29
30	.0004	.0003	.0002	.0002	.0002	.0001	.0001	30
31	.0003	.0002	.0002	.0001	.0001	.0001	.0001	31
32	.0002	.0002	.0001	.0001	.0001	.0001	.0001	32
33	.0002	.0001	.0001	.0001	.0001	.0001	.0000	33
34	.0001	.0001	.0001	.0001	.0000	.0000	.0000	34
35	.0001	.0001	.0001	.0000	.0000	.0000	.0000	35
36	.0001	.0001	.0000	.0000	.0000	.0000	.0000	36
37	.0001	.0000	.0000	.0000	.0000	.0000	.0000	37
38	.0000	.0000	.0000	.0000	.0000	.0000	.0000	38
39	.0000	.0000	.0000	.0000	.0000	.0000	.0000	39
40	.0000	.0000	.0000	.0000	.0000	.0000	.0000	40
41	.0000	.0000	.0000	.0000	.0000	.0000	.0000	41
42	.0000	.0000	.0000	.0000	.0000	.0000	.0000	42
43	.0000	.0000	.0000	.0000	.0000	.0000	.0000	43
44	.0000	.0000	.0000	.0000	.0000	.0000	.0000	44
45	.0000	.0000	.0000	.0000	.0000	.0000	.0000	45
46	.0000	.0000	.0000	.0000	.0000	.0000	.0000	46
47	.0000	.0000	.0000	.0000	.0000	.0000	.0000	47
48	.0000	.0000	.0000	.0000	.0000	.0000	.0000	48
49	.0000	.0000	.0000	.0000	.0000	.0000	.0000	49
50	.0000	.0000	.0000	.0000	.0000	.0000	.0000	50

TABLE A-1. PRESENT VALUE FACTORS (Continued)

PERIOD	37.0%	38.0%	39.0%	40.0%	41.0%	42.0%	43.0%	PERIOD
1	.7299	.7246	.7194	.7143	.7092	.7042	.6993	1
2	.5328	.5251	.5176	.5102	.5030	.4959	.4890	2
3	.3889	.3805	.3724	.3644	.3567	.3492	.3420	3
4	.2839	.2757	.2679	.2603	.2530	.2459	.2391	4
5	.2072	.1998	.1927	.1859	.1794	.1732	.1672	5
6	.1512	.1448	.1386	.1328	.1273	.1220	.1169	6
7	.1104	.1049	.0997	.0949	.0903	.0859	.0818	7
8	.0806	.0760	.0718	.0678	.0640	.0605	.0572	8
9	.0588	.0551	.0516	.0484	.0454	.0426	.0400	9
10	.0429	.0399	.0371	.0346	.0322	.0300	.0280	10
11	.0313	.0289	.0267	.0247	.0228	.0211	.0196	11
12	.0229	.0210	.0192	.0176	.0162	.0149	.0137	12
13	.0167	.0152	.0138	.0126	.0115	.0105	.0096	13
14	.0122	.0110	.0099	.0090	.0081	.0074	.0067	14
15	.0089	.0080	.0072	.0064	.0058	.0052	.0047	15
16	.0065	.0058	.0051	.0046	.0041	.0037	.0033	16
17	.0047	.0042	.0037	.0033	.0029	.0026	.0023	17
18	.0035	.0030	.0027	.0023	.0021	.0018	.0016	18
19	.0025	.0022	.0019	.0017	.0015	.0013	.0011	19
20	.0018	.0016	.0014	.0012	.0010	.0009	.0008	20
21	.0013	.0012	.0010	.0009	.0007	.0006	.0005	21
22	.0010	.0008	.0007	.0006	.0005	.0004	.0004	22
23	.0007	.0006	.0005	.0004	.0004	.0003	.0003	23
24	.0005	.0004	.0004	.0003	.0003	.0002	.0002	24
25	.0004	.0003	.0003	.0002	.0002	.0002	.0001	25
26	.0003	.0002	.0002	.0002	.0001	.0001	.0001	26
27	.0002	.0002	.0001	.0001	.0001	.0001	.0001	27
28	.0001	.0001	.0001	.0001	.0001	.0001	.0000	28
29	.0001	.0001	.0001	.0001	.0000	.0000	.0000	29
30	.0001	.0001	.0001	.0000	.0000	.0000	.0000	30
31	.0001	.0000	.0000	.0000	.0000	.0000	.0000	31
32	.0000	.0000	.0000	.0000	.0000	.0000	.0000	32
33	.0000	.0000	.0000	.0000	.0000	.0000	.0000	33
34	.0000	.0000	.0000	.0000	.0000	.0000	.0000	34
35	.0000	.0000	.0000	.0000	.0000	.0000	.0000	35
36	.0000	.0000	.0000	.0000	.0000	.0000	.0000	36
37	.0000	.0000	.0000	.0000	.0000	.0000	.0000	37
38	.0000	.0000	.0000	.0000	.0000	.0000	.0000	38
39	.0000	.0000	.0000	.0000	.0000	.0000	.0000	39
40	.0000	.0000	.0000	.0000	.0000	.0000	.0000	40
41	.0000	.0000	.0000	.0000	.0000	.0000	.0000	41
42	.0000	.0000	.0000	.0000	.0000	.0000	.0000	42
43	.0000	.0000	.0000	.0000	.0000	.0000	.0000	43
44	.0000	.0000	.0000	.0000	.0000	.0000	.0000	44
45	.0000	.0000	.0000	.0000	.0000	.0000	.0000	45
46	.0000	.0000	.0000	.0000	.0000	.0000	.0000	46
47	.0000	.0000	.0000	.0000	.0000	.0000	.0000	47
48	.0000	.0000	.0000	.0000	.0000	.0000	.0000	48
49	.0000	.0000	.0000	.0000	.0000	.0000	.0000	49
50	.0000	.0000	.0000	.0000	.0000	.0000	.0000	50

APPENDIX

TABLE A-1. PRESENT VALUE FACTORS (Continued)

PERIOD	44.0%	45.0%	46.0%	47.0%	48.0%	49.0%	50.0%	PERIOD
1	.6944	.6897	.6849	.6803	.6757	.6711	.6667	1
2	.4823	.4756	.4691	.4628	.4565	.4504	.4444	2
3	.3349	.3280	.3213	.3148	.3085	.3023	.2963	3
4	.2326	.2262	.2201	.2142	.2084	.2029	.1975	4
5	.1615	.1560	.1507	.1457	.1408	.1362	.1317	5
6	.1122	.1076	.1032	.0991	.0952	.0914	.0878	6
7	.0779	.0742	.0707	.0674	.0643	.0613	.0585	7
8	.0541	.0512	.0484	.0459	.0434	.0412	.0390	8
9	.0376	.0353	.0332	.0312	.0294	.0276	.0260	9
10	.0261	.0243	.0227	.0212	.0198	.0185	.0173	10
11	.0181	.0168	.0156	.0144	.0134	.0124	.0116	11
12	.0126	.0116	.0107	.0098	.0091	.0084	.0077	12
13	.0087	.0080	.0073	.0067	.0061	.0056	.0051	13
14	.0061	.0055	.0050	.0045	.0041	.0038	.0034	14
15	.0042	.0038	.0034	.0031	.0028	.0025	.0023	15
16	.0029	.0026	.0023	.0021	.0019	.0017	.0015	16
17	.0020	.0018	.0016	.0014	.0013	.0011	.0010	17
18	.0014	.0012	.0011	.0010	.0009	.0008	.0007	18
19	.0010	.0009	.0008	.0007	.0006	.0005	.0005	19
20	.0007	.0006	.0005	.0005	.0004	.0003	.0003	20
21	.0005	.0004	.0004	.0003	.0003	.0002	.0002	21
22	.0003	.0003	.0002	.0002	.0002	.0002	.0001	22
23	.0002	.0002	.0002	.0001	.0001	.0001	.0001	23
24	.0002	.0001	.0001	.0001	.0001	.0001	.0001	24
25	.0001	.0001	.0001	.0001	.0001	.0000	.0000	25
26	.0001	.0001	.0001	.0000	.0000	.0000	.0000	26
27	.0001	.0000	.0000	.0000	.0000	.0000	.0000	27
28	.0000	.0000	.0000	.0000	.0000	.0000	.0000	28
29	.0000	.0000	.0000	.0000	.0000	.0000	.0000	29
30	.0000	.0000	.0000	.0000	.0000	.0000	.0000	30
31	.0000	.0000	.0000	.0000	.0000	.0000	.0000	31
32	.0000	.0000	.0000	.0000	.0000	.0000	.0000	32
33	.0000	.0000	.0000	.0000	.0000	.0000	.0000	33
34	.0000	.0000	.0000	.0000	.0000	.0000	.0000	34
35	.0000	.0000	.0000	.0000	.0000	.0000	.0000	35
36	.0000	.0000	.0000	.0000	.0000	.0000	.0000	36
37	.0000	.0000	.0000	.0000	.0000	.0000	.0000	37
38	.0000	.0000	.0000	.0000	.0000	.0000	.0000	38
39	.0000	.0000	.0000	.0000	.0000	.0000	.0000	39
40	.0000	.0000	.0000	.0000	.0000	.0000	.0000	40
41	.0000	.0000	.0000	.0000	.0000	.0000	.0000	41
42	.0000	.0000	.0000	.0000	.0000	.0000	.0000	42
43	.0000	.0000	.0000	.0000	.0000	.0000	.0000	43
44	.0000	.0000	.0000	.0000	.0000	.0000	.0000	44
45	.0000	.0000	.0000	.0000	.0000	.0000	.0000	45
46	.0000	.0000	.0000	.0000	.0000	.0000	.0000	46
47	.0000	.0000	.0000	.0000	.0000	.0000	.0000	47
48	.0000	.0000	.0000	.0000	.0000	.0000	.0000	48
49	.0000	.0000	.0000	.0000	.0000	.0000	.0000	49
50	.0000	.0000	.0000	.0000	.0000	.0000	.0000	50

TABLE A-2. PRESENT VALUE OF ANNUITY FACTORS

PERIOD	0.0%	.5%	1.0%	1.5%	2.0%	PERIOD
1	1.0000	.9950	.9901	.9852	.9804	1
2	2.0000	1.9851	1.9704	1.9559	1.9416	2
3	3.0000	2.9702	2.9410	2.9122	2.8839	3
4	4.0000	3.9505	3.9020	3.8544	3.8077	4
5	5.0000	4.9259	4.8534	4.7826	4.7135	5
6	6.0000	5.8964	5.7955	5.6972	5.6014	6
7	7.0000	6.8621	6.7282	6.5982	6.4720	7
8	8.0000	7.8230	7.6517	7.4859	7.3255	8
9	9.0000	8.7791	8.5660	8.3605	8.1622	9
10	10.0000	9.7304	9.4713	9.2222	8.9826	10
11	11.0000	10.6770	10.3676	10.0711	9.7868	11
12	12.0000	11.6189	11.2551	10.9075	10.5753	12
13	13.0000	12.5562	12.1337	11.7315	11.3484	13
14	14.0000	13.4887	13.0037	12.5434	12.1062	14
15	15.0000	14.4166	13.8651	13.3432	12.8493	15
16	16.0000	15.3399	14.7179	14.1313	13.5777	16
17	17.0000	16.2586	15.5623	14.9076	14.2919	17
18	18.0000	17.1728	16.3983	15.6726	14.9920	18
19	19.0000	18.0824	17.2260	16.4262	15.6785	19
20	20.0000	18.9874	18.0456	17.1686	16.3514	20
21	21.0000	19.8880	18.8570	17.9001	17.0112	21
22	22.0000	20.7841	19.6604	18.6208	17.6580	22
23	23.0000	21.6757	20.4558	19.3309	18.2922	23
24	24.0000	22.5629	21.2434	20.0304	18.9139	24
25	25.0000	23.4456	22.0232	20.7196	19.5235	25
26	26.0000	24.3240	22.7952	21.3986	20.1210	26
27	27.0000	25.1980	23.5596	22.0676	20.7069	27
28	28.0000	26.0677	24.3164	22.7267	21.2813	28
29	29.0000	26.9330	25.0658	23.3761	21.8444	29
30	30.0000	27.7941	25.8077	24.0158	22.3965	30
31	31.0000	28.6508	26.5423	24.6461	22.9377	31
32	32.0000	29.5033	27.2696	25.2671	23.4683	32
33	33.0000	30.3515	27.9897	25.8790	23.9886	33
34	34.0000	31.1955	28.7027	26.4817	24.4986	34
35	35.0000	32.0354	29.4086	27.0756	24.9986	35
36	36.0000	32.8710	30.1075	27.6607	25.4888	36
37	37.0000	33.7025	30.7995	28.2371	25.9695	37
38	38.0000	34.5299	31.4847	28.8050	26.4406	38
39	39.0000	35.3531	32.1630	29.3646	26.9026	39
40	40.0000	36.1722	32.8347	29.9158	27.3555	40
41	41.0000	36.9873	33.4997	30.4590	27.7995	41
42	42.0000	37.7983	34.1581	30.9940	28.2348	42
43	43.0000	38.6053	34.8100	31.5212	28.6616	43
44	44.0000	39.4082	35.4555	32.0406	29.0800	44
45	45.0000	40.2072	36.0945	32.5523	29.4902	45
46	46.0000	41.0022	36.7272	33.0565	29.8923	46
47	47.0000	41.7932	37.3537	33.5532	30.2866	47
48	48.0000	42.5803	37.9740	34.0425	30.6731	48
49	49.0000	43.3635	38.5881	34.5247	31.0521	49
50	50.0000	44.1428	39.1961	34.9997	31.4236	50

TABLE A-2. PRESENT VALUE OF ANNUITY FACTORS (Continued)

PERIOD	2.5%	3.0%	3.5%	4.0%	4.5%	PERIOD
1	.9756	.9709	.9662	.9615	.9569	1
2	1.9274	1.9135	1.8997	1.8861	1.8727	2
3	2.8560	2.8286	2.8016	2.7751	2.7490	3
4	3.7620	3.7171	3.6731	3.6299	3.5875	4
5	4.6458	4.5797	4.5151	4.4518	4.3900	5
6	5.5081	5.4172	5.3286	5.2421	5.1579	6
7	6.3494	6.2303	6.1145	6.0021	5.8927	7
8	7.1701	7.0197	6.8740	6.7327	6.5959	8
9	7.9709	7.7861	7.6077	7.4353	7.2688	9
10	8.7521	8.5302	8.3166	8.1109	7.9127	10
11	9.5142	9.2526	9.0016	8.7605	8.5289	11
12	10.2578	9.9540	9.6633	9.3851	9.1186	12
13	10.9832	10.6350	10.3027	9.9856	9.6829	13
14	11.6909	11.2961	10.9205	10.5631	10.2228	14
15	12.3814	11.9379	11.5174	11.1184	10.7395	15
16	13.0550	12.5611	12.0941	11.6523	11.2340	16
17	13.7122	13.1661	12.6513	12.1657	11.7072	17
18	14.3534	13.7535	13.1897	12.6593	12.1600	18
19	14.9789	14.3238	13.7098	13.1339	12.5933	19
20	15.5892	14.8775	14.2124	13.5903	13.0079	20
21	16.1845	15.4150	14.6980	14.0292	13.4047	21
22	16.7654	15.9369	15.1671	14.4511	13.7844	22
23	17.3321	16.4436	15.6204	14.8568	14.1478	23
24	17.8850	16.9355	16.0584	15.2470	14.4955	24
25	18.4244	17.4131	16.4815	15.6221	14.8282	25
26	18.9506	17.8768	16.8904	15.9828	15.1466	26
27	19.4640	18.3270	17.2854	16.3296	15.4513	27
28	19.9649	18.7641	17.6670	16.6631	15.7429	28
29	20.4535	19.1885	18.0358	16.9837	16.0219	29
30	20.9303	19.6004	18.3920	17.2920	16.2889	30
31	21.3954	20.0004	18.7363	17.5885	16.5444	31
32	21.8492	20.3888	19.0689	17.8736	16.7889	32
33	22.2919	20.7658	19.3902	18.1476	17.0229	33
34	22.7238	21.1318	19.7007	18.4112	17.2468	34
35	23.1452	21.4872	20.0007	18.6646	17.4610	35
36	23.5562	21.8322	20.2905	18.9083	17.6660	36
37	23.9573	22.1672	20.5705	19.1426	17.8622	37
38	24.3486	22.4925	20.8411	19.3679	18.0500	38
39	24.7303	22.8082	21.1025	19.5845	18.2297	39
40	25.1028	23.1148	21.3551	19.7928	18.4016	40
41	25.4661	23.4124	21.5991	19.9930	18.5661	41
42	25.8206	23.7014	21.8349	20.1856	18.7235	42
43	26.1664	23.9819	22.0627	20.3708	18.8742	43
44	26.5038	24.2543	22.2828	20.5488	19.0184	44
45	26.8330	24.5187	22.4954	20.7200	19.1563	45
46	27.1542	24.7754	22.7009	20.8847	19.2884	46
47	27.4675	25.0247	22.8994	21.0429	19.4147	47
48	27.7732	25.2667	23.0912	21.1951	19.5356	48
49	28.0714	25.5017	23.2766	21.3415	19.6513	49
50	28.3623	25.7298	23.4556	21.4822	19.7620	50

TABLE A-2. PRESENT VALUE OF ANNUITY FACTORS (Continued)

PERIOD	5.0%	5.5%	6.0%	6.5%	7.0%	PERIOD
1	.9524	.9479	.9434	.9390	.9346	1
2	1.8594	1.8463	1.8334	1.8206	1.8080	2
3	2.7232	2.6979	2.6730	2.6485	2.6243	3
4	3.5460	3.5051	3.4651	3.4258	3.3872	4
5	4.3295	4.2703	4.2124	4.1557	4.1002	5
6	5.0757	4.9955	4.9173	4.8410	4.7665	6
7	5.7864	5.6830	5.5824	5.4845	5.3893	7
8	6.4632	6.3346	6.2098	6.0888	5.9713	8
9	7.1078	6.9522	6.8017	6.6561	6.5152	9
10	7.7217	7.5376	7.3601	7.1888	7.0236	10
11	8.3064	8.0925	7.8869	7.6890	7.4987	11
12	8.8633	8.6185	8.3838	8.1587	7.9427	12
13	9.3936	9.1171	8.8527	8.5997	8.3576	13
14	9.8986	9.5896	9.2950	9.0138	8.7455	14
15	10.3797	10.0376	9.7122	9.4027	9.1079	15
16	10.8378	10.4622	10.1059	9.7678	9.4466	16
17	11.2741	10.8646	10.4773	10.1106	9.7632	17
18	11.6896	11.2461	10.8276	10.4325	10.0591	18
19	12.0853	11.6077	11.1581	10.7347	10.3356	19
20	12.4622	11.9504	11.4699	11.0185	10.5940	20
21	12.8212	12.2752	11.7641	11.2850	10.8355	21
22	13.1630	12.5832	12.0416	11.5352	11.0612	22
23	13.4886	12.8750	12.3034	11.7701	11.2722	23
24	13.7986	13.1517	12.5504	11.9907	11.4693	24
25	14.0939	13.4139	12.7834	12.1979	11.6536	25
26	14.3752	13.6625	13.0032	12.3924	11.8258	26
27	14.6430	13.8981	13.2105	12.5750	11.9867	27
28	14.8981	14.1214	13.4062	12.7465	12.1371	28
29	15.1411	14.3331	13.5907	12.9075	12.2777	29
30	15.3724	14.5337	13.7648	13.0587	12.4090	30
31	15.5928	14.7239	13.9291	13.2006	12.5318	31
32	15.8027	14.9042	14.0840	13.3339	12.6466	32
33	16.0025	15.0751	14.2302	13.4591	12.7538	33
34	16.1929	15.2370	14.3681	13.5766	12.8540	34
35	16.3742	15.3906	14.4982	13.6870	12.9477	35
36	16.5468	15.5361	14.6210	13.7906	13.0352	36
37	16.7113	15.6740	14.7368	13.8879	13.1170	37
38	16.8679	15.8047	14.8460	13.9792	13.1935	38
39	17.0170	15.9287	14.9491	14.0650	13.2649	39
40	17.1591	16.0461	15.0463	14.1455	13.3317	40
41	17.2944	16.1575	15.1380	14.2212	13.3941	41
42	17.4232	16.2630	15.2245	14.2922	13.4524	42
43	17.5459	16.3630	15.3062	14.3588	13.5070	43
44	17.6628	16.4578	15.3832	14.4214	13.5579	44
45	17.7741	16.5477	15.4558	14.4802	13.6055	45
46	17.8801	16.6329	15.5244	14.5354	13.6500	46
47	17.9810	16.7137	15.5890	14.5873	13.6916	47
48	18.0772	16.7902	15.6500	14.6359	13.7305	48
49	18.1687	16.8628	15.7076	14.6816	13.7668	49
50	18.2559	16.9315	15.7619	14.7245	13.8007	50

TABLE A-2. PRESENT VALUE OF ANNUITY FACTORS (Continued)

PERIOD	7.5%	8.0%	8.5%	9.0%	9.5%	PERIOD
1	.9302	.9259	.9217	.9174	.9132	1
2	1.7956	1.7833	1.7711	1.7591	1.7473	2
3	2.6005	2.5771	2.5540	2.5313	2.5089	3
4	3.3493	3.3121	3.2756	3.2397	3.2045	4
5	4.0459	3.9927	3.9406	3.8897	3.8397	5
6	4.6938	4.6229	4.5536	4.4859	4.4198	6
7	5.2966	5.2064	5.1185	5.0330	4.9496	7
8	5.8573	5.7466	5.6392	5.5348	5.4334	8
9	6.3789	6.2469	6.1191	5.9952	5.8753	9
10	6.8641	6.7101	6.5613	6.4177	6.2788	10
11	7.3154	7.1390	6.9690	6.8052	6.6473	11
12	7.7353	7.5361	7.3447	7.1607	6.9838	12
13	8.1258	7.9038	7.6910	7.4869	7.2912	13
14	8.4892	8.2442	8.0101	7.7861	7.5719	14
15	8.8271	8.5595	8.3042	8.0607	7.8282	15
16	9.1415	8.8514	8.5753	8.3126	8.0623	16
17	9.4340	9.1216	8.8252	8.5436	8.2760	17
18	9.7060	9.3719	9.0555	8.7556	8.4713	18
19	9.9591	9.6036	9.2677	8.9501	8.6496	19
20	10.1945	9.8181	9.4633	9.1285	8.8124	20
21	10.4135	10.0168	9.6436	9.2922	8.9611	21
22	10.6172	10.2007	9.8098	9.4424	9.0969	22
23	10.8067	10.3711	9.9629	9.5802	9.2209	23
24	10.9830	10.5288	10.1041	9.7066	9.3341	24
25	11.1469	10.6748	10.2342	9.8226	9.4376	25
26	11.2995	10.8100	10.3541	9.9290	9.5320	26
27	11.4414	10.9352	10.4646	10.0266	9.6183	27
28	11.5734	11.0511	10.5665	10.1161	9.6971	28
29	11.6962	11.1584	10.6603	10.1983	9.7690	29
30	11.8104	11.2578	10.7468	10.2737	9.8347	30
31	11.9166	11.3498	10.8266	10.3428	9.8947	31
32	12.0155	11.4350	10.9001	10.4062	9.9495	32
33	12.1074	11.5139	10.9678	10.4644	9.9996	33
34	12.1929	11.5869	11.0302	10.5178	10.0453	34
35	12.2725	11.6546	11.0878	10.5668	10.0870	35
36	12.3465	11.7172	11.1408	10.6118	10.1251	36
37	12.4154	11.7752	11.1897	10.6530	10.1599	37
38	12.4794	11.8289	11.2347	10.6908	10.1917	38
39	12.5390	11.8786	11.2763	10.7255	10.2207	39
40	12.5944	11.9246	11.3145	10.7574	10.2472	40
41	12.6460	11.9672	11.3498	10.7866	10.2715	41
42	12.6939	12.0067	11.3823	10.8134	10.2936	42
43	12.7385	12.0432	11.4123	10.8379	10.3138	43
44	12.7800	12.0771	11.4399	10.8605	10.3322	44
45	12.8186	12.1084	11.4653	10.8812	10.3490	45
46	12.8545	12.1374	11.4888	10.9002	10.3644	46
47	12.8879	12.1643	11.5104	10.9176	10.3785	47
48	12.9190	12.1891	11.5303	10.9336	10.3913	48
49	12.9479	12.2122	11.5487	10.9482	10.4030	49
50	12.9748	12.2335	11.5656	10.9617	10.4137	50

TABLE A-2. PRESENT VALUE OF ANNUITY FACTORS (Continued)

PERIOD	10.0%	10.5%	11.0%	11.5%	12.0%	PERIOD
1	.9091	.9050	.9009	.8969	.8929	1
2	1.7355	1.7240	1.7125	1.7012	1.6901	2
3	2.4869	2.4651	2.4437	2.4226	2.4018	3
4	3.1699	3.1359	3.1024	3.0696	3.0373	4
5	3.7908	3.7429	3.6959	3.6499	3.6048	5
6	4.3553	4.2972	4.2305	4.1703	4.1114	6
7	4.8684	4.7893	4.7122	4.6370	4.5638	7
8	5.3349	5.2392	5.1461	5.0556	4.9676	8
9	5.7590	5.6463	5.5370	5.4311	5.3282	9
10	6.1446	6.0148	5.8892	5.7678	5.6502	10
11	6.4951	6.3482	6.2065	6.0697	5.9377	11
12	6.8137	6.6500	6.4924	6.3406	6.1944	12
13	7.1034	6.9230	6.7499	6.5835	6.4235	13
14	7.3667	7.1702	6.9819	6.8013	6.6282	14
15	7.6061	7.3938	7.1909	6.9967	6.8109	15
16	7.8237	7.5962	7.3792	7.1719	6.9740	16
17	8.0216	7.7794	7.5488	7.3291	7.1196	17
18	8.2014	7.9451	7.7016	7.4700	7.2497	18
19	8.3649	8.0952	7.8393	7.5964	7.3658	19
20	8.5136	8.2309	7.9633	7.7098	7.4694	20
21	8.6487	8.3538	8.0751	7.8115	7.5620	21
22	8.7715	8.4649	8.1757	7.9027	7.6446	22
23	8.8832	8.5656	8.2664	7.9845	7.7184	23
24	8.9847	8.6566	8.3481	8.0578	7.7843	24
25	9.0770	8.7390	8.4217	8.1236	7.8431	25
26	9.1609	8.8136	8.4881	8.1826	7.8957	26
27	9.2372	8.8811	8.5478	8.2355	7.9426	27
28	9.3066	8.9422	8.6016	8.2830	7.9844	28
29	9.3696	8.9974	8.6501	8.3255	8.0218	29
30	9.4269	9.0474	8.6938	8.3637	8.0552	30
31	9.4790	9.0927	8.7331	8.3979	8.0850	31
32	9.5264	9.1337	8.7686	8.4287	8.1116	32
33	9.5694	9.1707	8.8005	8.4562	8.1354	33
34	9.6086	9.2043	8.8293	8.4809	8.1566	34
35	9.6442	9.2347	8.8552	8.5030	8.1755	35
36	9.6765	9.2621	8.8786	8.5229	8.1924	36
37	9.7059	9.2870	8.8996	8.5407	8.2075	37
38	9.7327	9.3095	8.9186	8.5567	8.2210	38
39	9.7570	9.3299	8.9357	8.5710	8.2330	39
40	9.7790	9.3483	8.9510	8.5839	8.2438	40
41	9.7991	9.3650	8.9649	8.5954	8.2534	41
42	9.8174	9.3801	8.9774	8.6058	8.2619	42
43	9.8340	9.3937	8.9886	8.6150	8.2696	43
44	9.8491	9.4061	8.9988	8.6233	8.2764	44
45	9.8628	9.4173	9.0079	8.6308	8.2825	45
46	9.8753	9.4274	9.0161	8.6375	8.2880	46
47	9.8866	9.4366	9.0235	8.6435	8.2928	47
48	9.8969	9.4448	9.0302	8.6489	8.2972	48
49	9.9063	9.4523	9.0362	8.6537	8.3010	49
50	9.9148	9.4591	9.0417	8.6580	8.3045	50

TABLE A-2. PRESENT VALUE OF ANNUITY FACTORS (Continued)

PERIOD	12.5%	13.0%	13.5%	14.0%	14.5%	PERIOD
1	.8889	.8850	.8811	.8772	.8734	1
2	1.6790	1.6681	1.6573	1.6467	1.6361	2
3	2.3813	2.3612	2.3412	2.3216	2.3023	3
4	3.0056	2.9745	2.9438	2.9137	2.8841	4
5	3.5606	3.5172	3.4747	3.4331	3.3922	5
6	4.0538	3.9975	3.9425	3.8887	3.8360	6
7	4.4923	4.4226	4.3546	4.2883	4.2236	7
8	4.8820	4.7988	4.7177	4.6389	4.5621	8
9	5.2285	5.1317	5.0377	4.9464	4.8577	9
10	5.5364	5.4262	5.3195	5.2161	5.1159	10
11	5.8102	5.6869	5.5679	5.4527	5.3414	11
12	6.0535	5.9176	5.7867	5.6603	5.5383	12
13	6.2698	6.1218	5.9794	5.8424	5.7103	13
14	6.4620	6.3025	6.1493	6.0021	5.8606	14
15	6.6329	6.4624	6.2989	6.1422	5.9918	15
16	6.7848	6.6039	6.4308	6.2651	6.1063	16
17	6.9198	6.7291	6.5469	6.3729	6.2064	17
18	7.0398	6.8399	6.6493	6.4674	6.2938	18
19	7.1465	6.9380	6.7395	6.5504	6.3701	19
20	7.2414	7.0248	6.8189	6.6231	6.4368	20
21	7.3256	7.1015	6.8889	6.6870	6.4950	21
22	7.4006	7.1695	6.9506	6.7429	6.5459	22
23	7.4672	7.2297	7.0049	6.7921	6.5903	23
24	7.5264	7.2829	7.0528	6.8351	6.6291	24
25	7.5790	7.3300	7.0950	6.8729	6.6629	25
26	7.6258	7.3717	7.1321	6.9061	6.6925	26
27	7.6674	7.4086	7.1649	6.9352	6.7184	27
28	7.7043	7.4412	7.1937	6.9607	6.7409	28
29	7.7372	7.4701	7.2191	6.9830	6.7606	29
30	7.7664	7.4957	7.2415	7.0027	6.7778	30
31	7.7923	7.5183	7.2613	7.0199	6.7929	31
32	7.8154	7.5383	7.2786	7.0350	6.8060	32
33	7.8359	7.5560	7.2940	7.0482	6.8175	33
34	7.8541	7.5717	7.3075	7.0599	6.8275	34
35	7.8704	7.5856	7.3193	7.0700	6.8362	35
36	7.8848	7.5979	7.3298	7.0790	6.8439	36
37	7.8976	7.6087	7.3390	7.0868	6.8505	37
38	7.9089	7.6183	7.3472	7.0937	6.8564	38
39	7.9191	7.6268	7.3543	7.0997	6.8615	39
40	7.9281	7.6344	7.3607	7.1050	6.8659	40
41	7.9361	7.6410	7.3662	7.1097	6.8698	41
42	7.9432	7.6469	7.3711	7.1138	6.8732	42
43	7.9495	7.6522	7.3754	7.1173	6.8761	43
44	7.9551	7.6568	7.3792	7.1205	6.8787	44
45	7.9601	7.6609	7.3826	7.1232	6.8810	45
46	7.9645	7.6645	7.3855	7.1256	6.8829	46
47	7.9685	7.6677	7.3881	7.1277	6.8847	47
48	7.9720	7.6705	7.3904	7.1296	6.8862	48
49	7.9751	7.6730	7.3924	7.1312	6.8875	49
50	7.9778	7.6752	7.3942	7.1327	6.8886	50

TABLE A-2. PRESENT VALUE OF ANNUITY FACTORS (Continued)

PERIOD	15.0%	15.5%	16.0%	16.5%	17.0%	PERIOD
1	.8696	.8658	.8621	.8584	.8547	1
2	1.6257	1.6154	1.6052	1.5952	1.5852	2
3	2.2832	2.2644	2.2459	2.2276	2.2096	3
4	2.8550	2.8263	2.7982	2.7705	2.7432	4
5	3.3522	3.3129	3.2743	3.2365	3.1993	5
6	3.7845	3.7341	3.6847	3.6365	3.5892	6
7	4.1604	4.0988	4.0386	3.9798	3.9224	7
8	4.4873	4.4145	4.3436	4.2745	4.2072	8
9	4.7716	4.6879	4.6065	4.5275	4.4506	9
10	5.0188	4.9246	4.8332	4.7446	4.6586	10
11	5.2337	5.1295	5.0286	4.9310	4.8364	11
12	5.4206	5.3069	5.1971	5.0910	4.9884	12
13	5.5831	5.4605	5.3423	5.2283	5.1183	13
14	5.7245	5.5935	5.4675	5.3462	5.2293	14
15	5.8474	5.7087	5.5755	5.4474	5.3242	15
16	5.9542	5.8084	5.6685	5.5342	5.4053	16
17	6.0472	5.8947	5.7487	5.6088	5.4746	17
18	6.1280	5.9695	5.8178	5.6728	5.5339	18
19	6.1982	6.0342	5.8775	5.7277	5.5845	19
20	6.2593	6.0902	5.9288	5.7748	5.6278	20
21	6.3125	6.1387	5.9731	5.8153	5.6648	21
22	6.3587	6.1807	6.0113	5.8501	5.6964	22
23	6.3988	6.2170	6.0442	5.8799	5.7234	23
24	6.4338	6.2485	6.0726	5.9055	5.7465	24
25	6.4641	6.2758	6.0971	5.9274	5.7662	25
26	6.4906	6.2994	6.1182	5.9463	5.7831	26
27	6.5135	6.3198	6.1364	5.9625	5.7975	27
28	6.5335	6.3375	6.1520	5.9764	5.8099	28
29	6.5509	6.3528	6.1656	5.9883	5.8204	29
30	6.5660	6.3661	6.1772	5.9986	5.8294	30
31	6.5791	6.3775	6.1872	6.0073	5.8371	31
32	6.5905	6.3875	6.1959	6.0149	5.8437	32
33	6.6005	6.3961	6.2034	6.0214	5.8493	33
34	6.6091	6.4035	6.2098	6.0269	5.8541	34
35	6.6166	6.4100	6.2153	6.0317	5.8582	35
36	6.6231	6.4156	6.2201	6.0358	5.8617	36
37	6.6288	6.4204	6.2242	6.0393	5.8647	37
38	6.6338	6.4246	6.2278	6.0423	5.8673	38
39	6.6380	6.4282	6.2309	6.0449	5.8695	39
40	6.6418	6.4314	6.2335	6.0471	5.8713	40
41	6.6450	6.4341	6.2358	6.0490	5.8729	41
42	6.6478	6.4364	6.2377	6.0507	5.8743	42
43	6.6503	6.4385	6.2394	6.0521	5.8755	43
44	6.6524	6.4402	6.2409	6.0533	5.8765	44
45	6.6543	6.4418	6.2421	6.0543	5.8773	45
46	6.6559	6.4431	6.2432	6.0552	5.8781	46
47	6.6573	6.4442	6.2442	6.0560	5.8787	47
48	6.6585	6.4452	6.2450	6.0566	5.8792	48
49	6.6596	6.4461	6.2457	6.0572	5.8797	49
50	6.6605	6.4468	6.2463	6.0577	5.8801	50

154

TABLE A-2. PRESENT VALUE OF ANNUITY FACTORS (Continued)

PERIOD	17.5%	18.0%	18.5%	19.0%	20.0%	PERIOD
1	.8511	.8475	.8439	.8403	.8333	1
2	1.5754	1.5656	1.5560	1.5465	1.5278	2
3	2.1918	2.1743	2.1570	2.1399	2.1065	3
4	2.7164	2.6901	2.6641	2.6386	2.5887	4
5	3.1629	3.1272	3.0921	3.0576	2.9906	5
6	3.5429	3.4976	3.4532	3.4098	3.3255	6
7	3.8663	3.8115	3.7580	3.7057	3.6046	7
8	4.1415	4.0776	4.0152	3.9544	3.8372	8
9	4.3758	4.3030	4.2322	4.1633	4.0310	9
10	4.5751	4.4941	4.4154	4.3389	4.1925	10
11	4.7448	4.6560	4.5699	4.4865	4.3271	11
12	4.8892	4.7932	4.7004	4.6105	4.4392	12
13	5.0121	4.9095	4.8104	4.7147	4.5327	13
14	5.1167	5.0081	4.9033	4.8023	4.6106	14
15	5.2057	5.0916	4.9817	4.8759	4.6755	15
16	5.2814	5.1624	5.0479	4.9377	4.7296	16
17	5.3459	5.2223	5.1037	4.9897	4.7746	17
18	5.4008	5.2732	5.1508	5.0333	4.8122	18
19	5.4475	5.3162	5.1905	5.0700	4.8435	19
20	5.4872	5.3527	5.2241	5.1009	4.8696	20
21	5.5210	5.3837	5.2524	5.1268	4.8913	21
22	5.5498	5.4099	5.2763	5.1486	4.9094	22
23	5.5743	5.4321	5.2964	5.1668	4.9245	23
24	5.5951	5.4509	5.3134	5.1822	4.9371	24
25	5.6129	5.4669	5.3278	5.1951	4.9476	25
26	5.6280	5.4804	5.3399	5.2060	4.9563	26
27	5.6408	5.4919	5.3501	5.2151	4.9636	27
28	5.6518	5.5016	5.3588	5.2228	4.9697	28
29	5.6611	5.5098	5.3661	5.2292	4.9747	29
30	5.6690	5.5168	5.3722	5.2347	4.9789	30
31	5.6758	5.5227	5.3774	5.2392	4.9824	31
32	5.6815	5.5277	5.3818	5.2430	4.9854	32
33	5.6864	5.5320	5.3854	5.2462	4.9878	33
34	5.6905	5.5356	5.3886	5.2489	4.9898	34
35	5.6941	5.5386	5.3912	5.2512	4.9915	35
36	5.6971	5.5412	5.3934	5.2531	4.9929	36
37	5.6996	5.5434	5.3953	5.2547	4.9941	37
38	5.7018	5.5452	5.3969	5.2561	4.9951	38
39	5.7037	5.5468	5.3982	5.2572	4.9959	39
40	5.7053	5.5482	5.3993	5.2582	4.9966	40
41	5.7066	5.5493	5.4003	5.2590	4.9972	41
42	5.7077	5.5502	5.4011	5.2596	4.9976	42
43	5.7087	5.5510	5.4017	5.2602	4.9980	43
44	5.7096	5.5517	5.4023	5.2607	4.9984	44
45	5.7103	5.5523	5.4028	5.2611	4.9986	45
46	5.7109	5.5528	5.4032	5.2614	4.9989	46
47	5.7114	5.5532	5.4036	5.2617	4.9991	47
48	5.7118	5.5536	5.4038	5.2619	4.9992	48
49	5.7122	5.5539	5.4041	5.2621	4.9993	49
50	5.7125	5.5541	5.4043	5.2623	4.9994	50

TABLE A-2. PRESENT VALUE OF ANNUITY FACTORS (Continued)

PERIOD	21.0%	22.0%	23.0%	24.0%	25.0%	PERIOD
1	.8264	.8197	.8130	.8065	.8000	1
2	1.5095	1.4915	1.4740	1.4568	1.4400	2
3	2.0739	2.0422	2.0114	1.9813	1.9520	3
4	2.5404	2.4936	2.4483	2.4043	2.3616	4
5	2.9260	2.8636	2.8035	2.7454	2.6893	5
6	3.2446	3.1669	3.0923	3.0205	2.9514	6
7	3.5079	3.4155	3.3270	3.2423	3.1611	7
8	3.7256	3.6193	3.5179	3.4212	3.3289	8
9	3.9054	3.7863	3.6731	3.5655	3.4631	9
10	4.0541	3.9232	3.7993	3.6819	3.5705	10
11	4.1769	4.0354	3.9018	3.7757	3.6564	11
12	4.2784	4.1274	3.9852	3.8514	3.7251	12
13	4.3624	4.2028	4.0530	3.9124	3.7801	13
14	4.4317	4.2646	4.1082	3.9616	3.8241	14
15	4.4890	4.3152	4.1530	4.0013	3.8593	15
16	4.5364	4.3567	4.1894	4.0333	3.8874	16
17	4.5755	4.3908	4.2190	4.0591	3.9099	17
18	4.6079	4.4187	4.2431	4.0799	3.9279	18
19	4.6346	4.4415	4.2627	4.0967	3.9424	19
20	4.6567	4.4603	4.2786	4.1103	3.9539	20
21	4.6750	4.4756	4.2916	4.1212	3.9631	21
22	4.6900	4.4882	4.3021	4.1300	3.9705	22
23	4.7025	4.4985	4.3106	4.1371	3.9764	23
24	4.7128	4.5070	4.3176	4.1428	3.9811	24
25	4.7213	4.5139	4.3232	4.1474	3.9849	25
26	4.7284	4.5196	4.3278	4.1511	3.9879	26
27	4.7342	4.5243	4.3316	4.1542	3.9903	27
28	4.7390	4.5281	4.3346	4.1566	3.9923	28
29	4.7430	4.5312	4.3371	4.1585	3.9938	29
30	4.7463	4.5338	4.3391	4.1601	3.9950	30
31	4.7490	4.5359	4.3407	4.1614	3.9960	31
32	4.7512	4.5376	4.3421	4.1624	3.9968	32
33	4.7531	4.5390	4.3431	4.1632	3.9975	33
34	4.7546	4.5402	4.3440	4.1639	3.9980	34
35	4.7559	4.5411	4.3447	4.1644	3.9984	35
36	4.7569	4.5419	4.3453	4.1649	3.9987	36
37	4.7578	4.5426	4.3458	4.1652	3.9990	37
38	4.7585	4.5431	4.3462	4.1655	3.9992	38
39	4.7591	4.5435	4.3465	4.1657	3.9993	39
40	4.7596	4.5439	4.3467	4.1659	3.9995	40
41	4.7600	4.5441	4.3469	4.1660	3.9996	41
42	4.7603	4.5444	4.3471	4.1662	3.9997	42
43	4.7606	4.5446	4.3472	4.1663	3.9997	43
44	4.7608	4.5447	4.3473	4.1663	3.9998	44
45	4.7610	4.5449	4.3474	4.1664	3.9998	45
46	4.7612	4.5450	4.3475	4.1665	3.9999	46
47	4.7613	4.5451	4.3476	4.1665	3.9999	47
48	4.7614	4.5451	4.3476	4.1665	3.9999	48
49	4.7615	4.5452	4.3477	4.1666	3.9999	49
50	4.7616	4.5452	4.3477	4.1666	3.9999	50

TABLE A-2. PRESENT VALUE OF ANNUITY FACTORS (Continued)

PERIOD	26.0%	27.0%	28.0%	29.0%	30.0%	PERIOD
1	.7937	.7874	.7813	.7752	.7692	1
2	1.4235	1.4074	1.3916	1.3761	1.3609	2
3	1.9234	1.8956	1.8684	1.8420	1.8161	3
4	2.3202	2.2800	2.2410	2.2031	2.1662	4
5	2.6351	2.5827	2.5320	2.4830	2.4356	5
6	2.8850	2.8210	2.7594	2.7000	2.6427	6
7	3.0833	3.0087	2.9370	2.8682	2.8021	7
8	3.2407	3.1564	3.0758	2.9986	2.9247	8
9	3.3657	3.2728	3.1842	3.0997	3.0190	9
10	3.4648	3.3644	3.2689	3.1781	3.0915	10
11	3.5435	3.4365	3.3351	3.2388	3.1473	11
12	3.6059	3.4933	3.3868	3.2859	3.1903	12
13	3.6555	3.5381	3.4272	3.3224	3.2233	13
14	3.6949	3.5733	3.4587	3.3507	3.2487	14
15	3.7261	3.6010	3.4834	3.3726	3.2682	15
16	3.7509	3.6228	3.5026	3.3896	3.2832	16
17	3.7705	3.6400	3.5177	3.4028	3.2948	17
18	3.7861	3.6536	3.5294	3.4130	3.3037	18
19	3.7985	3.6642	3.5386	3.4210	3.3105	19
20	3.8083	3.6726	3.5458	3.4271	3.3158	20
21	3.8161	3.6792	3.5514	3.4319	3.3198	21
22	3.8223	3.6844	3.5558	3.4356	3.3230	22
23	3.8273	3.6885	3.5592	3.4384	3.3253	23
24	3.8312	3.6918	3.5619	3.4406	3.3272	24
25	3.8342	3.6943	3.5640	3.4423	3.3286	25
26	3.8367	3.6963	3.5656	3.4437	3.3297	26
27	3.8387	3.6979	3.5669	3.4447	3.3305	27
28	3.8402	3.6991	3.5679	3.4455	3.3312	28
29	3.8414	3.7001	3.5687	3.4461	3.3317	29
30	3.8424	3.7009	3.5693	3.4466	3.3321	30
31	3.8432	3.7015	3.5697	3.4470	3.3324	31
32	3.8438	3.7019	3.5701	3.4473	3.3326	32
33	3.8443	3.7023	3.5704	3.4475	3.3328	33
34	3.8447	3.7026	3.5706	3.4477	3.3329	34
35	3.8450	3.7028	3.5708	3.4478	3.3330	35
36	3.8452	3.7030	3.5709	3.4479	3.3331	36
37	3.8454	3.7032	3.5710	3.4480	3.3331	37
38	3.8456	3.7033	3.5711	3.4481	3.3332	38
39	3.8457	3.7034	3.5712	3.4481	3.3332	39
40	3.8458	3.7034	3.5712	3.4481	3.3332	40
41	3.8459	3.7035	3.5713	3.4482	3.3333	41
42	3.8459	3.7035	3.5713	3.4482	3.3333	42
43	3.8460	3.7036	3.5713	3.4482	3.3333	43
44	3.8460	3.7036	3.5714	3.4482	3.3333	44
45	3.8460	3.7036	3.5714	3.4482	3.3333	45
46	3.8461	3.7036	3.5714	3.4482	3.3333	46
47	3.8461	3.7037	3.5714	3.4483	3.3333	47
48	3.8461	3.7037	3.5714	3.4483	3.3333	48
49	3.8461	3.7037	3.5714	3.4483	3.3333	49
50	3.8461	3.7037	3.5714	3.4483	3.3333	50

TABLE A-2. PRESENT VALUE OF ANNUITY FACTORS (Continued)

PERIOD	31.0%	32.0%	33.0%	34.0%	35.0%	PERIOD
1	.7634	.7576	.7519	.7463	.7407	1
2	1.3461	1.3315	1.3172	1.3032	1.2894	2
3	1.7909	1.7663	1.7423	1.7188	1.6959	3
4	2.1305	2.0957	2.0618	2.0290	1.9969	4
5	2.3897	2.3452	2.3021	2.2604	2.2200	5
6	2.5875	2.5342	2.4828	2.4331	2.3852	6
7	2.7386	2.6775	2.6187	2.5620	2.5075	7
8	2.8539	2.7860	2.7208	2.6582	2.5982	8
9	2.9419	2.8681	2.7976	2.7300	2.6653	9
10	3.0091	2.9304	2.8553	2.7836	2.7150	10
11	3.0604	2.9776	2.8987	2.8236	2.7519	11
12	3.0995	3.0133	2.9314	2.8534	2.7792	12
13	3.1294	3.0404	2.9559	2.8757	2.7994	13
14	3.1522	3.0609	2.9744	2.8923	2.8144	14
15	3.1696	3.0764	2.9883	2.9047	2.8255	15
16	3.1829	3.0882	2.9987	2.9140	2.8337	16
17	3.1931	3.0971	3.0065	2.9209	2.8398	17
18	3.2008	3.1039	3.0124	2.9260	2.8443	18
19	3.2067	3.1090	3.0169	2.9299	2.8476	19
20	3.2112	3.1129	3.0202	2.9327	2.8501	20
21	3.2147	3.1158	3.0227	2.9349	2.8519	21
22	3.2173	3.1180	3.0246	2.9365	2.8533	22
23	3.2193	3.1197	3.0260	2.9377	2.8543	23
24	3.2209	3.1210	3.0271	2.9386	2.8550	24
25	3.2220	3.1220	3.0279	2.9392	2.8556	25
26	3.2229	3.1227	3.0285	2.9397	2.8560	26
27	3.2236	3.1233	3.0289	2.9401	2.8563	27
28	3.2241	3.1237	3.0293	2.9404	2.8565	28
29	3.2245	3.1240	3.0295	2.9406	2.8567	29
30	3.2248	3.1242	3.0297	2.9407	2.8568	30
31	3.2251	3.1244	3.0299	2.9408	2.8569	31
32	3.2252	3.1246	3.0300	2.9409	2.8569	32
33	3.2254	3.1247	3.0301	2.9410	2.8570	33
34	3.2255	3.1248	3.0301	2.9410	2.8570	34
35	3.2256	3.1248	3.0302	2.9411	2.8571	35
36	3.2256	3.1249	3.0302	2.9411	2.8571	36
37	3.2257	3.1249	3.0302	2.9411	2.8571	37
38	3.2257	3.1249	3.0302	2.9411	2.8571	38
39	3.2257	3.1249	3.0303	2.9411	2.8571	39
40	3.2257	3.1250	3.0303	2.9412	2.8571	40
41	3.2258	3.1250	3.0303	2.9412	2.8571	41
42	3.2258	3.1250	3.0303	2.9412	2.8571	42
43	3.2258	3.1250	3.0303	2.9412	2.8571	43
44	3.2258	3.1250	3.0303	2.9412	2.8571	44
45	3.2258	3.1250	3.0303	2.9412	2.8571	45
46	3.2258	3.1250	3.0303	2.9412	2.8571	46
47	3.2258	3.1250	3.0303	2.9412	2.8571	47
48	3.2258	3.1250	3.0303	2.9412	2.8571	48
49	3.2258	3.1250	3.0303	2.9412	2.8571	49
50	3.2258	3.1250	3.0303	2.9412	2.8571	50

TABLE A-2. PRESENT VALUE OF ANNUITY FACTORS (Continued)

PERIOD	36.0%	37.0%	38.0%	39.0%	40.0%	PERIOD
1	.7353	.7299	.7246	.7194	.7143	1
2	1.2760	1.2627	1.2497	1.2370	1.2245	2
3	1.6735	1.6516	1.6302	1.6093	1.5889	3
4	1.9658	1.9355	1.9060	1.8772	1.8492	4
5	2.1807	2.1427	2.1058	2.0699	2.0352	5
6	2.3388	2.2939	2.2506	2.2086	2.1680	6
7	2.4550	2.4043	2.3555	2.3083	2.2628	7
8	2.5404	2.4849	2.4315	2.3801	2.3306	8
9	2.6033	2.5437	2.4866	2.4317	2.3790	9
10	2.6495	2.5867	2.5265	2.4689	2.4136	10
11	2.6834	2.6180	2.5555	2.4956	2.4383	11
12	2.7084	2.6409	2.5764	2.5148	2.4559	12
13	2.7268	2.6576	2.5916	2.5286	2.4685	13
14	2.7403	2.6698	2.6026	2.5386	2.4775	14
15	2.7502	2.6787	2.6106	2.5457	2.4839	15
16	2.7575	2.6852	2.6164	2.5509	2.4885	16
17	2.7629	2.6899	2.6206	2.5546	2.4918	17
18	2.7668	2.6934	2.6236	2.5573	2.4941	18
19	2.7697	2.6959	2.6258	2.5592	2.4958	19
20	2.7718	2.6977	2.6274	2.5606	2.4970	20
21	2.7734	2.6991	2.6285	2.5616	2.4979	21
22	2.7746	2.7000	2.6294	2.5623	2.4985	22
23	2.7754	2.7008	2.6300	2.5628	2.4989	23
24	2.7760	2.7013	2.6304	2.5632	2.4992	24
25	2.7765	2.7017	2.6307	2.5634	2.4994	25
26	2.7768	2.7019	2.6310	2.5636	2.4996	26
27	2.7771	2.7022	2.6311	2.5637	2.4997	27
28	2.7773	2.7023	2.6313	2.5638	2.4998	28
29	2.7774	2.7024	2.6313	2.5639	2.4999	29
30	2.7775	2.7025	2.6314	2.5640	2.4999	30
31	2.7776	2.7025	2.6315	2.5640	2.4999	31
32	2.7776	2.7026	2.6315	2.5640	2.4999	32
33	2.7777	2.7026	2.6315	2.5641	2.5000	33
34	2.7777	2.7026	2.6315	2.5641	2.5000	34
35	2.7777	2.7027	2.6315	2.5641	2.5000	35
36	2.7777	2.7027	2.6316	2.5641	2.5000	36
37	2.7777	2.7027	2.6316	2.5641	2.5000	37
38	2.7778	2.7027	2.6316	2.5641	2.5000	38
39	2.7778	2.7027	2.6316	2.5641	2.5000	39
40	2.7778	2.7027	2.6316	2.5641	2.5000	40
41	2.7778	2.7027	2.6316	2.5641	2.5000	41
42	2.7778	2.7027	2.6316	2.5641	2.5000	42
43	2.7778	2.7027	2.6316	2.5641	2.5000	43
44	2.7778	2.7027	2.6316	2.5641	2.5000	44
45	2.7778	2.7027	2.6316	2.5641	2.5000	45
46	2.7778	2.7027	2.6316	2.5641	2.5000	46
47	2.7778	2.7027	2.6316	2.5641	2.5000	47
48	2.7778	2.7027	2.6316	2.5641	2.5000	48
49	2.7778	2.7027	2.6316	2.5641	2.5000	49
50	2.7778	2.7027	2.6316	2.5641	2.5000	50

TABLE A-2. PRESENT VALUE OF ANNUITY FACTORS (Continued)

PERIOD	41.0%	42.0%	43.0%	44.0%	45.0%	PERIOD
1	.7092	.7042	.6993	.6944	.6897	1
2	1.2122	1.2002	1.1883	1.1767	1.1653	2
3	1.5689	1.5494	1.5303	1.5116	1.4933	3
4	1.8219	1.7954	1.7694	1.7442	1.7195	4
5	2.0014	1.9686	1.9367	1.9057	1.8755	5
6	2.1286	2.0905	2.0536	2.0178	1.9831	6
7	2.2189	2.1764	2.1354	2.0957	2.0573	7
8	2.2829	2.2369	2.1926	2.1498	2.1085	8
9	2.3283	2.2795	2.2326	2.1874	2.1438	9
10	2.3605	2.3095	2.2605	2.2134	2.1681	10
11	2.3833	2.3307	2.2801	2.2316	2.1849	11
12	2.3995	2.3455	2.2938	2.2441	2.1965	12
13	2.4110	2.3560	2.3033	2.2529	2.2045	13
14	2.4192	2.3634	2.3100	2.2589	2.2100	14
15	2.4249	2.3686	2.3147	2.2632	2.2138	15
16	2.4290	2.3722	2.3180	2.2661	2.2164	16
17	2.4319	2.3748	2.3203	2.2681	2.2182	17
18	2.4340	2.3766	2.3219	2.2695	2.2195	18
19	2.4355	2.3779	2.3230	2.2705	2.2203	19
20	2.4365	2.3788	2.3238	2.2712	2.2209	20
21	2.4372	2.3794	2.3243	2.2717	2.2213	21
22	2.4378	2.3799	2.3247	2.2720	2.2216	22
23	2.4381	2.3802	2.3250	2.2722	2.2218	23
24	2.4384	2.3804	2.3251	2.2724	2.2219	24
25	2.4386	2.3806	2.3253	2.2725	2.2220	25
26	2.4387	2.3807	2.3254	2.2726	2.2221	26
27	2.4388	2.3808	2.3254	2.2726	2.2221	27
28	2.4389	2.3808	2.3255	2.2726	2.2222	28
29	2.4389	2.3809	2.3255	2.2727	2.2222	29
30	2.4389	2.3809	2.3255	2.2727	2.2222	30
31	2.4390	2.3809	2.3255	2.2727	2.2222	31
32	2.4390	2.3809	2.3256	2.2727	2.2222	32
33	2.4390	2.3809	2.3256	2.2727	2.2222	33
34	2.4390	2.3809	2.3256	2.2727	2.2222	34
35	2.4390	2.3809	2.3256	2.2727	2.2222	35
36	2.4390	2.3809	2.3256	2.2727	2.2222	36
37	2.4390	2.3809	2.3256	2.2727	2.2222	37
38	2.4390	2.3809	2.3256	2.2727	2.2222	38
39	2.4390	2.3809	2.3256	2.2727	2.2222	39
40	2.4390	2.3810	2.3256	2.2727	2.2222	40
41	2.4390	2.3810	2.3256	2.2727	2.2222	41
42	2.4390	2.3810	2.3256	2.2727	2.2222	42
43	2.4390	2.3810	2.3256	2.2727	2.2222	43
44	2.4390	2.3810	2.3256	2.2727	2.2222	44
45	2.4390	2.3810	2.3256	2.2727	2.2222	45
46	2.4390	2.3810	2.3256	2.2727	2.2222	46
47	2.4390	2.3810	2.3256	2.2727	2.2222	47
48	2.4390	2.3810	2.3256	2.2727	2.2222	48
49	2.4390	2.3810	2.3256	2.2727	2.2222	49
50	2.4390	2.3810	2.3256	2.2727	2.2222	50

TABLE A-2. PRESENT VALUE OF ANNUITY FACTORS (Continued)

PERIOD	46.0%	47.0%	48.0%	49.0%	50.0%	PERIOD
1	.6849	.6803	.6757	.6711	.6667	1
2	1.1541	1.1430	1.1322	1.1216	1.1111	2
3	1.4754	1.4579	1.4407	1.4239	1.4074	3
4	1.6955	1.6720	1.6491	1.6268	1.6049	4
5	1.8462	1.8177	1.7899	1.7629	1.7366	5
6	1.9495	1.9168	1.8851	1.8543	1.8244	6
7	2.0202	1.9842	1.9494	1.9156	1.8829	7
8	2.0686	2.0301	1.9928	1.9568	1.9220	8
9	2.1018	2.0613	2.0222	1.9844	1.9480	9
10	2.1245	2.0825	2.0420	2.0030	1.9653	10
11	2.1401	2.0969	2.0554	2.0154	1.9769	11
12	2.1507	2.1068	2.0645	2.0238	1.9846	12
13	2.1580	2.1134	2.0706	2.0294	1.9897	13
14	2.1630	2.1180	2.0747	2.0331	1.9931	14
15	2.1665	2.1211	2.0775	2.0357	1.9954	15
16	2.1688	2.1232	2.0794	2.0374	1.9970	16
17	2.1704	2.1246	2.0807	2.0385	1.9980	17
18	2.1715	2.1256	2.0815	2.0393	1.9986	18
19	2.1723	2.1263	2.0821	2.0398	1.9991	19
20	2.1728.	2.1267	2.0825	2.0401	1.9994	20
21	2.1731	2.1270	2.0828	2.0403	1.9996	21
22	2.1734	2.1272	2.0830	2.0405	1.9997	22
23	2.1736	2.1274	2.0831	2.0406	1.9998	23
24	2.1737	2.1275	2.0832	2.0407	1.9999	24
25	2.1737	2.1275	2.0832	2.0407	1.9999	25
26	2.1738	2.1276	2.0833	2.0408	1.9999	26
27	2.1738	2.1276	2.0833	2.0408	2.0000	27
28	2.1739	2.1276	2.0833	2.0408	2.0000	28
29	2.1739	2.1276	2.0833	2.0408	2.0000	29
30	2.1739	2.1276	2.0833	2.0408	2.0000	30
31	2.1739	2.1276	2.0833	2.0408	2.0000	31
32	2.1739	2.1276	2.0833	2.0408	2.0000	32
33	2.1739	2.1277	2.0833	2.0408	2.0000	33
34	2.1739	2.1277	2.0833	2.0408	2.0000	34
35	2.1739	2.1277	2.0833	2.0408	2.0000	35
36	2.1739	2.1277	2.0833	2.0408	2.0000	36
37	2.1739	2.1277	2.0833	2.0408	2.0000	37
38	2.1739	2.1277	2.0833	2.0408	2.0000	38
39	2.1739	2.1277	2.0833	2.0408	2.0000	39
40	2.1739	2.1277	2.0833	2.0408	2.0000	40
41	2.1739	2.1277	2.0833	2.0408	2.0000	41
42	2.1739	2.1277	2.0833	2.0408	2.0000	42
43	2.1739	2.1277	2.0833	2.0408	2.0000	43
44	2.1739	2.1277	2.0833	2.0408	2.0000	44
45	2.1739	2.1277	2.0833	2.0408	2.0000	45
46	2.1739	2.1277	2.0833	2.0408	2.0000	46
47	2.1739	2.1277	2.0833	2.0408	2.0000	47
48	2.1739	2.1277	2.0833	2.0408	2.0000	48
49	2.1739	2.1277	2.0833	2.0408	2.0000	49
50	2.1739	2.1277	2.0833	2.0408	2.0000	50